Alan C. Elms
1974

Dimensions of a New Identity

BY ERIK H. ERIKSON

Childhood and Society (1950, 1963)
Young Man Luther (1958)
Insight and Responsibility (1964)
Identity: Youth and Crisis (1968)
Gandhi's Truth (1969)
Dimensions of a New Identity (1974)
In Search of Common Ground (1973)
(with Huey P. Newton and
Kai T. Erikson)

ERIK H. ERIKSON

Dimensions
of a
New Identity:

The 1973 Jefferson Lectures
in the Humanities

W · W · NORTON & COMPANY · INC ·
New York

Library of Congress Cataloging in Publication Data

Erikson, Erik Homburger, 1902–
  Dimensions of a new identity.

  (Jefferson lectures in the humanities, 1973)
1. Jefferson, Thomas, Pres. U.S., 1743–1826.
2. Identity (Psychology) I. Title. II. Series:
Jefferson lecture in the humanities, 1973.
E332.2.E74   973.4'6'0924 [B]   73–22289
ISBN 0–393–05515–9

Contents

Preface

WHEN THE National Endowment for the Humanities announced a yearly Jefferson lecture, it attached to the occasion, besides the illustrious name, expectations which are beyond the hope of fulfillment of any but a very few individuals, be they from a "scholarly, creative, public, or scientific walk of life." These expectations range from "humanistic insights of importance" to "living issues as the test of humane learning." A visit from the then acting chairman of the Endowment, Wallace Edgerton, set my apprehensions sufficiently at rest so that, in preparation for the lectures, I could permit my mind to wander over issues prominent in Jefferson's life and sayings which were, at the time, also essential to further clarification in my area of work.

In the Washington of May Day, 1973, however, when the first lecture was delivered, humanistic insights and public issues (at least of the more sensational kind) seemed to have parted ways as never before, and this in a striking inner-political sequence to the nation's division over the war in Southeast Asia. Predictably, some of the audience of the Jefferson lectures expected a clarification of living issues as contemporary as the day before and after. I deemed it inadvisable, however, to let short-range perspective dictate the nature of the Jefferson lectures, especially since I found it difficult enough to fit the thoughts prepared into the time allotted. Since then the long-range convergence of contemporary concerns with my main themes has become clearer and I have attempted to spell this out as I enlarged the lectures for this printed version. I have endeavored, however, for the most part to maintain a spoken rather than a written style. These, then, are still two lectures given on successive evenings. In order to interrupt such a lengthy discourse (as speakers are in a position to do, when with a sudden, alert "Ladies and Gentlemen" they manage to reawaken both the audience and themselves) I have provided my text with subtitles. I hope that this will allow the readers to shift in their chairs and to join me in periodic new starts from different perspectives.

As personal an experience as the Jefferson lectures are for the lecturer, they are part of a yearly occasion: This year the Endowment brought together its national representatives and legislative sponsors. I want to express my thanks to the chairman, Dr. Ronald S. Berman, and his staff for the way in which they helped me to play a central, if passing, role on one such impressive occasion. If my lectures make a limited contribution from the standpoint of a particular lifework, subsequent speakers will amplify and give perspective to earlier ones, and the whole lectureship become a lively addition to the Endowment's work, so essential for our national life.

I

The Founders:
Jeffersonian Action and Faith

Introduction: From Case History to History

In fairness to the Endowment, I should first of all declare —with my gratitude for this invitation—my awareness of the fact that Thomas Jefferson was to be the guiding spirit of these lectures, but by no means necessarily the subject. Yet, I was drawn to take a new look at Thomas Jefferson, and (as I should have known) once you look at him, it is impossible to get around him. But, as the best have found out, it is equally hard to get *at* him. Jefferson's image, it has been said often enough, has so many facets that I must begin by paraphrasing John F. Kennedy's famous remark, made to an assembly of Nobel Prize winners in the White House, that no equally "extraordinary collection of talent, of human knowledge" had been gathered there since President Jefferson dined alone. One could say with equal justice that, brilliantly studied as he has been by devoted scholars (and, of course, also hastily analyzed by many more occasional reviewers), this man still walks through time as an enigmatic figure whose image is amplified as successive generations attempt to behold him. I consider myself, then, a witness before a perpetual assembly of scholars, feeling called upon to represent a particular viewpoint dictated by a circumscribed competence as an American and a professional.

I am an immigrant belatedly catching up with what (supposedly) every American youngster learns in school about this country's history. And yet, there is much about Jefferson's transplantation of a classical stance to this continent which my humanist education in Europe prepared me to appreciate. But I am also an old man who in speaking tonight realizes that the theoretical orientation he brought with him from Europe has taken on in this country a direction which, for whatever it is worth, could have taken root only here: Wherefore my title, unashamedly, connects my identity concepts with this occasion.

And finally, there is an issue to be settled. I am a psychoanalyst and, as some of you know, my name is often associated with the term "*psychohistory*." Now, I would wish it understood from the outset, that I have come to use this term only with tacit quotation marks. For while the unadorned term on early occasions came rather naturally —as once did *psychobiology* or *psychosomatics* until we found that such terminology perpetuates the very split it means to deny—I would not wish to associate myself with all that is done in the name of this term. Therefore, a few brief words on methodology seem indicated so that I can proceed to tell you in my own way how I would go about approaching a historical figure like Jefferson.

Psychohistory, essentially, is the study of individual and collective life with the combined methods of psychoanalysis and history. In spite of, or because of, the very special and conflicting demands made on the practitioners of these two fields, bridgeheads must be built on each side in order to make a true span possible. But the completed bridge should permit unimpeded two-way traffic; and once this is done, history will simply be history again, but now a history aware of the fact that it has always indulged in a covert and circuitous traffic with psychology which can now be direct, overt, and aware. By the same token, psychoanalysis will have become conscious of its own historical determinants, and *case history* and *life history* will no longer be manners of speaking. The way you "take history" is also a way of "making history."

Because of the clinical origin of psychoanalysis, however, what is now called psychohistory often tends to resemble a case history. A genuine case history gives an account of what went wrong with a person and of why the person fell apart or stopped developing; it attempts to assign to the particular malfunctioning a diagnosis in line with the observer's psychodynamic views; and it arrives at therapeutic suggestions as to what could or can be done to reactivate a sounder development in this and in similar cases. A life history, in contrast, describes how a person managed to keep together and to maintain a significant function in the lives of others. ~~The hero of a life history, of course, usually has a chronic neurotic conflict as a significant function in the lives of others.~~ The hero of a life history, of course, usually has a chronic neurotic conflict as a significant part of his whole make-up but he becomes a case only insofar as the conflict has him.

When I made my first foray into this field, I was annoyed as much as amused about the regularity with which the reviews, both in England and here, were captioned "Luther on the Couch." Since then, I have read some analyses of great figures (including Jefferson) which, indeed, treated what these persons said or wrote as if their utterances had been free associations in the course of more or less voluntary confessions and admissions of the kind patients make in the clinical context. This is simply bad methodology. The life history of a historical figure, instead, must take account, above all, of how his life hung together even as he also kept a section of his world together. His person, then, in all its uniqueness and yet also in its conflictedness and failures, must be seen, for better and for worse, as prototypical for his time and as fulfilling specific needs in the lives of those who followed him.

The fact that psychohistorical work, however, has had some roots in psychoanalysis, has lasting consequences of great significance. For one, the psychoanalyst, in his training, must learn in principle to understand in himself such unconscious motivation as he analyzes in others. To this purpose, he undergoes a training psychoanalysis. And in helping his patient to find out what can (and did) go wrong in his life, he must promote what in the patient's own nature is ready to heal itself. Thus, he must learn not only to do no harm, but, in fact, not to use interpretation in order to advance his own idealizations or condemnations—not, at any rate, without knowing and acknowledging systematically that he is doing it, and why.

A corresponding Hippocratic responsibility in psychohistory is easy to see, but much harder to formulate and to agree on: Who has (and what constitutes) the training to "diagnose" historical figures and, in a new sense, to "doctor" history? The lawfulness we seek in studying the life history of a historical person must at the same time clarify his personal aims in terms of those of his times, and relate both him and his times to the psychohistorian's values. Good historians, I would think, have always expressed, in style as well as in judgment, some awareness of their own place in history. For history is not only the record of the inter-actions between leaders and led which bring about lasting changes in political power and in the power of ideas, it is also a record of how historical concepts influence as well as reflect both the writing and the making of history. As such awareness is sharpened by psychological insight, and as, at the same time, leaders and led, with the eager inter-vention of the media, become more self-conscious in every sense of the word, new responsibilities arise, which I would consider an apt and mandatory subject for that consortium of scholars and scientists studying Jefferson's life and times before whom I will now appear as a witness.

To sum up with Daniel Boorstin, "Our past must serve us not as an anthology from which to call apt phrases for current needs, but as a stage for observing, in all their tantalizing complexity, the actual ways in which men have faced the ancient problems of the human race." To which a psychoanalyst will add that the past here must include the early life of individuals as well as that of the race, and that, in both, "ancient problems" are apt to prove astonish-ingly contemporary, indeed.

The View from Monticello

But now let us attempt to catch a glimpse of the way the world looked to Jefferson. I will call this "The View from Monticello." As Dumas Malone has pointed out, Jefferson was studied for a whole century primarily as a great *statesman*, a life history synonymous with the creation of the new nation, and only then as a great *humanist*, a man who in his private as well as in public life cultivated a renewal of ancient values on a new continent. Only in our own time has his enigmatic and conflicted *personality* been studied systematically; and more of this to come.

From what I have said so far about my motives and my mandate, it must be clear that I could make a contribution only in an inverse direction: from the study of Jefferson's developing personality, to his humanism, and finally to his statesmanship. But, as I indicated, even a statesman's most

idiosyncratic style of action (unless it is openly symptomatic of a breakdown of personal control) always reflects
existing conditions and moods, and especially conditions-
in-the-making—which include his own intentions. One
must, then, study the intricate workings of history as well
as of the man if one is to mark the personality of a statesman. And to find access to his inner workings one must
once more, review all the data available for the significant
selections and possibly suggestive omissions by previous
workers. Nothing, I know now, could be more interesting to do; and I would, no doubt, have done so if I had
been asked a decade ago to give the Jefferson Lectures
in 1973. As it is, I must select the kind of material most
accessible to me. I will concentrate today on two of Jefferson's literary works: first, his only book, namely, the *Notes
on the State of Virginia* which, as you will see, are a model
of psychohistorical writing in that they not only account
for the state of his state, but also for his own state as an
observer. And I will review a second book, his edition of
the New Testament, the Gospels according to Thomas
Jefferson, president of the United States.

Jefferson was thirty-eight years old when he wrote the
Notes on the State of Virginia, and his book is essentially
a survey—statistical and geographic—of his then much
larger state which, as a good colonist, he called "my country." But his outlook is that from Monticello, that resi-
dence elevated above all other plantation homes in the area,
and overlooking the Blue Ridge Mountains. Jefferson had
inherited it from his father, together with forests and fields,
slaves and "other movable property." It may have been his
father who had called it Monticello, but, if I may say so,
I have never been comfortable with the translation "little

mountain" which neither fits the contour nor the accrued significance of the place. *Monte*, in fact, means "mount" and can refer to an elevation having more significance than its height would justify—as is implied in the Sermon on the Mount as well as in *Acro-polis*—both of which I hope to connect with the meaning of Monticello.

It is all too easy for the casual visitor to see Monticello as an aristocratic plantation home elevated only by its master's design and fortune above those of the aristocrats who had, in Jefferson's words, "seated themselves below the tide water on the main rivers" and "lived in a style of luxury and extravagance." The fact is that it became a distinct kind of architectural manifesto. Nor did Jefferson think much of the aristocratic line of succession: His neighbors' less-endowed descendants he came to call "half-breeds." Even below these, however, he ranked the "pretenders," those who attempted to act like aristocrats and to "detach themselves from the plebeian ranks." He believed in a "natural aristocracy" to be based on the "solid and independent yeomanry" whose confidence was based on the competence of work and the power of faith. At any rate, Monticello, as built and ceaselessly rebuilt by him, was meant to be above his society as well as to be above its habitual settlements; and if Jefferson could later say of the University of Virginia (which he planned within view of Monticello) that it was to be "the future bulwark of the human mind in this hemisphere," one may well understand that Monticello, before that, had assumed the character of a domed shrine where classical style and European learning would be renewed and united with that homegrown American naturalness which was to bring the best out of cultivated nature—including human nature. If this is what

Monticello stands for and what Americans now view with nostalgia, they know (or sense) that in Jefferson's own lifetime, "the age of ornament," in the words of his friend William Wirt, was to be over; that of "utility" was to succeed. In the meantime, however, it is important to recognize the dominance of the identity element of the *natural aristocrat* which came to Jefferson from the father's side. If the fact that his father had married into the Randolph family and its inherited wealth, caused conflicts in the son, he yet seems to have received clear directions from the father's unbroken belief in self-improvement through work and study, as well as a fierce independence of spirit, going back to Welsh recalcitrance.

Jefferson had also inherited from his father, surveyor and prospector, his manly, tall, and lanky stature, with yet so sensitive features; and, in fact, the very passion to survey both the details in what is near and the boundaries of the horizon. I will not hesitate to nominate *surveyor* for another essential element in his identity, which was to assume national significance later in the Louisiana Purchase, and the inspired expeditions of Lewis and Clark.

As to the struggle of contrasting images in Jefferson's identity formation, listen to what, as president, he wrote to his grandson about his role choices: "Many a time have I asked myself in the enthusiastic moments of the death of a fox, the victory of a favorite horse, the issue of a question eloquently argued at the bar, or in the great council of the nation—well, which of these kinds of reputations should I prefer?" And he assures his correspondent that "these little returns into ourselves, this self-catechizing habit is not trifling nor useless, but leads to the prudent selection and steady pursuit of what is right." As you can see, however, even in his most introspective mood, the choices envisaged are all consummations crowning some kind of excellence. Interestingly, even as he was to become many things exceedingly well, he never was an eloquent orator; he *wrote* with supreme oratory. But it is good in old age to think one preferred not to be what one was not meant to be.

Now, at the age of thirty-eight in 1781, when he wrote the *Notes on the State of Virginia*, Jefferson had already authored the two immortal statements which he later chose to have noted on his tombstone as "testimonials that I have lived," namely, the *Declaration of Independence* and the draft of a *Statute of Virginia for Religious Freedom*. At the time of writing the *Notes*, however, he had reached the lowest point in his career. A wartime governor of his invaded state, and threatened with impeachment for having bungled some emergency measures, he was, in fact, a fugitive from Monticello, itself briefly occupied by the British. But it seems that Jefferson the writer was at his best and most personal when he was troubled; and the French diplomat who had asked him for a factual report, instead received a singularly eloquent document—which, if by a fluke of fate was not begun at Monticello, certainly represented the world as seen from there.

The *Notes*, then, for the most part, are a survey of geographic features, productive capacities, and population statistics: There were then three hundred thousand free inhabitants and, we must note, an almost equal number of slaves in Virginia. They also cover institutions and what he captions as "Manners," which we would call mores or culture today. Most of it is intensely practical; and all the more impressive are the emotional themes and, with them, major identity elements that sovereignly break through the accounting of facts.

There is, first of all, what I would identify as the element of *amateur*, the lover in the wider sense, here a lover of natural views. ("I feel, therefore I am," Jefferson would come to say.) One wonders, just for example, what, of all people, a Frenchman thought of such sensuousness as the following passage reveals: "Going out into the open air in the temperate and in the warm months of the year, we often meet with bodies of warm air which, passing by us in two or three seconds, do not afford time to the most sensible thermometer to seize their temperature. Judging from my feelings only I think they approach the ordinary heat of the human body. Some of them perhaps go a little beyond it—But whence taken? Where from? Or how generated?—They are most frequent about sunsets, rare in the middle parts of the day, and I do not recollect having ever met with them in the morning." "Met with them;" it is indeed like an intimate rendezvous, and yet the naturalist keeps his observing, his questioning distance.

And then there is a description of the famous natural wonder, the Natural Bridge and his reaction to it. He admits that this item is "not comprehended under the present head"; yet, as the "most sublime of Nature's works," it "must not be pretermitted. It is on the ascent of a hill, which seems to have been cloven through its lengths by some great convulsion. . . . Though the sides of this bridge are provided in some parts with a parapet of fixed rocks, yet few men have resolution to walk to them and look over into the abyss. You involuntarily fall on your hands and feet, creep to the parapet and peep over it." What follows, certainly is more detail than the Frenchman bargained for: "Looking down from this height about a minute gave me a violent headache—if the view from the top be painful and intolerable, that from below is delightful and an equal extreme. It is impossible for the emotions arising from the sublime to be felt beyond what they are here."

Jefferson later noted a certain confusion in his memory; but the point to be made is that in surveying the state of the State of Virginia, he includes an account of his personal state while doing the survey—a prime requirement for psychohistory. Note, if you please, for future reference the juxtaposition of height and downfall, of sublime emotions —and the violent pain in the head.

If Jefferson here freely reveals the symptom which later in the form of severe migraine was to mark the limit of his psychosomatic endurance, he confronts himself and us with his most unresolvable psychosocial conflict where another identity element finds expression. The *ideologue*, here at odds with what he remained all his life, a slave-holder, exclaims, "The laws do not permit us to turn the slaves loose if that were for their good, and to commute them for other property is to commit them to those whose usage of them we cannot control." And then he conveys a passionate insight that represents the *educator* so descriptively and so knowingly that it will occupy us in these lectures more than once. "There must doubtless be an unhappy influence on the manners of our people," he writes, "produced by the existence of slavery among us. . . . Our children see this, and learn to imitate it; for man is an imitative animal. . . . From his cradle to his grave he is learning to do what he sees others do. If a parent could find no motive either in his philanthropy or his self-love, for restraining the intemperance of passion toward his slave, it should always be a sufficient one that his child is present. But generally it is not sufficient. The parent storms, the child looks on, catches the lineaments of wrath, puts on the same airs in the circle of smaller slaves, gives a loose to his worst of passions, and thus nursed, educated, and daily exercised in tyranny, cannot but be stamped by it with odious peculiarities."

But, alas, in these *Notes* we are also faced with an effusive statement on the superiority of the white race which I would call unblushing if it did not make the very point that blushing is beautiful. Jefferson compares the fine mixtures of red and white and the "suffusions of colour" in the faces of the white race to the immovable veil of darkness which covers black faces and he points admiringly to the general "elegant symmetry" of the white form, and the flowing hair surrounding the face. He quotes the then widespread claim that the blacks themselves prefer whites; and here he must mean white women, for he compares this tendency, in turn, to the preference of the orang-utan (then widely believed to be a wild man-creature from the woods) for black women. There follows a long list of black inferiorities, culminating in a deficiency of qualities located in the head—a black could scarcely be capable of comprehending the investigations of Euclid—while conceding the powers of the heart. And yet, while "they are ardent after their female, love does not seem with them a tender, delicate mixture of sentiment and sensation."

Even these cursory excerpts will make it evident that the frank confusion of this discourse enables the modern moralist to assert (especially with the use of isolated quotations) that Jefferson here reveals personal idiosyncracies

of tenacious depth. And yet, the whole tone makes his own
protests credible that his remarks were only "hazarded
with great diffidence," and as doubts he hoped to find disproved.

In the balance, I would think that this Virginian must
be credited with facing, and facing "in all its tantalizing
complexity," one of the "ancient" problems of the human
race. For the question whether and why God had created
all men equal and had then let climate and geography dis-
criminate against some, was a question at once theological,
scientific, and ideological. Dr. Benjamin Rush, Jefferson's
physician-friend, whom we will quote repeatedly as the
closest to being a professional ancestor of ours in the
Jeffersonian circle and, in fact, a founding father of American psychiatry, solved this question neatly in diagnosing
all blacks as descendants of an African population once
ravaged by a gigantic epidemic of leprosy and therefore
differentiated only by disease from the common origin of
all mankind, which was the—naturally white—pair in the
Garden of Eden. Blackness called for medical intervention
and treatment, then, and with it for a "double portion of
our humanity." If Jefferson, in the meantime, warned
against miscegenation and tentatively advocated coloniza-
tion, this word, it should be remembered, then reflected
the official term *colonies* for what later became the American states and meant to guarantee to the ex-slaves the status
of a "free and independant people."

I will later return to the question of how these and other
aspects of Jefferson's identity (such as the *designer*) hung
together. Here we must take account of the combination
of ideological condemnation, scientific ridicule, and (more
recently) psychiatric diagnosis which have trailed these

last-quoted utterances. After his book had been published, Jefferson would come to agree with what he called a well-known prayer, "Oh, that mine *enemy* would write a book!"—a prayer which today is so readily granted to workers in the humanities—and, indeed, psychiatry. For who, so Jefferson rightly implies, could write a book on these issues without trapping himself in conflicting feelings and, if he were honest, in abhorred convictions, even if he could manage to sound ever so pure ideologically? The fact is that the matter of man's division into different races has by no means been resolved even today by staunch ideological means, either here at home or (one suspects) in the major revolutions abroad. It would seem to call, therefore, for psychological insights available only in our day—insights which make "mankind's ancient problems" amenable to each observer's self-awareness in a changing scientific and ideological climate.

New World, New Species

LET ME, THEN, present (once more) a concept of mine which is, I think, essential for an understanding of the intricate connection between man's bondage in ancient prejudices and his search for new identities. I mean the concept of *pseudospeciation* which deals with the fact, that all through history groups of men have entertained systematic illusions regarding the God-given superiority of their own kind.

But it occurs to me that I have not offered you as yet some kind of formula for the elusive subject of identity which appears in the very title of these lectures. Well, then: A sense of identity means a sense of being at one with oneself as one grows and develops; and it means, at the same time, a sense of affinity with a community's sense of being at one with its future as well as its history—or mythology. This formula we are about to apply to the new identity created on this continent by our founding fathers. They did not use this word, of course, and it would be more historical to speak instead of the new man. But what would you emphasize, *new* man which underscores newness, or new *man*, which promises a new mankind? And there are, today, good reasons for avoiding the word *man* where it might seem to exclude—or, indeed, carelessly include—women.

But these very questions only underline some of what is implicit in the problem of identity. And since you would expect a psychoanalyst to speak of what is implicit, and since some of you, at any rate, expect this analyst to speak of identity, we probably are where we should be. This concept, furthermore, is meant to include some complex and even sinister themes which we must not shirk: and here we come back to pseudospeciation. The *pseudo* means that, far from perceiving or accepting a human identity based on a common specieshood, different tribes and nations, creeds and classes (and, perchance, political parties) consider themselves to be the one chosen species and will, especially in times of crisis, sacrifice to this claim much of the knowledge, the logic, and the ethics that are theirs.

But when I proposed this term *pseudospeciation* in the very headquarters of Darwinism, in the Royal Society in London, I had no idea how florid, manifest, and indeed, conscious was this trend in pre-Darwinian days and in fact, in Jefferson's time.

Linnaeus, the great naturalist, had divided the species man into two groups: *Homo Diurnus*—that's all of us— and *Homo Nocturnus*, of whom the orangutan was a prime example. So it was a kind of homo that Jefferson (and others) had in mind when he spoke of that creature's preference for black women. *Homo Diurnus*, in turn, had a European, an Asiatic, an African, and American branch now vastly complicated by the fact that some European expatriates were settling on the land of the American aborigines and were importing Africans. In Jefferson's time, a "scientific" battle was on as to which of these branches had the tallest stature and the most sublime mind, and besides all those qualities associated with height and brain power, the best generative equipment endowed with the appropriate "ardor."

In this scientific warfare, the aboriginal as well as the colonial Americans fared badly. All creatures, so claimed especially the great French naturalist, the Count de Buffon, were getting smaller on the American continent, reduced in number, and diminished in ardor. "By refusing the American aborigines the power of love, nature has treated him," so Buffon insisted, "worse and lowered him deeper than any animal." The mammoth, Jefferson retorted and demonstrated with fossils collected at great expense and shipped to France, was native to America, and was it not the biggest animal that ever lived? Contradicting Buffon with other observations, he claimed that in this instance the great man's judgment had been "seduced by a glowing pen." But this is exactly our question: What kind of fervor makes an otherwise cool observer's pen glow? There was an Abbé de Raynal who went Buffon one better: He applied these theories to the new immigrants to the American continent, warned them of unavoidable degeneracy and in the kindness of his heart advised them to learn "how to make themselves happy with mediocrity" and "never to expect genius and never to be disappointed."

All this, if one can imagine it, was said to that new nation which was getting ready to devote itself to the very pursuit of happiness—and no inferior brand at that—by total independence and resolute action. Dr. Rush did not hesitate to advance the theory that what we would call a morale factor entered here, and that the invigorating influence of liberty would bring "animal life" to a perfect state—and here he meant animal spirit, or at any rate, some kind of psychosomatic vitality. He challenged the French to contrast the inhabitants of England and America with the Turks who lived under the despotism of the Ottoman Empire. Yet this social theory remained in conflict with the assumption that natural, not acquired, differences make some men love freedom. Jefferson himself thought conservatism to be an inborn quality, too. Commending tolerance, he claimed that even in America "the sickly, the weakly, the timid man *fears* the people and is a *Tory* by nature, while the healthy, strong, and *bold* man cherishes the people and is formed [sic] a *Whig* by nature." Yet Rush persisted that under the new conditions of liberty many of the children of Tory parents were going to be Whigs; and so, he added mysteriously, were the Jews in all the states.

Benjamin Franklin knew how to settle the matter. When both Jefferson and he were in Paris, he gave a party at Passy where one-half of the guests, invited to sit on one side of the table, were Americans, the other half French. And among the last was the Abbé de Raynal. When Franklin offered a toast, he asked both parties to rise, adding, "We will see on which side nature has degenerated," and it happened, of course, that his American guests were of the finest stature and form, while those of the other side were remarkably diminutive and the Abbé himself, as Jefferson recorded, was a "mere shrimp." As you see, even where we make peace among our own subspecies, we tend to belittle the shrimp, although a shrimp seems to be every bit tall enough to be a shrimp. It speaks for Franklin the host that he himself was probably on the small side among the Americans.

Darwin, by clarifying the origins of specieshood, including man's, forced the whole matter of pseudospeciation, here expressed in such chauvinist naturalism, deeper into the unconscious. I will return later to the psychological reasons for the need, on mankind's part, to maintain what we may call a certain cosmocentricity, that is to consider itself an original creation (Darwin took care of that) centrally located in the universe (as Copernicus successfully disproved) and ethnically elect and alone conscious of its will and purpose—that is, ethno- as well as egocentric. It is clear that just because we now know where we come from, we deep down—and this is the point I will come back to—do not believe a word of it. In fact, after Darwin we had the age of holocausts to prove not only the superiority of one pseudospecies over another but also its right to exterminate the other by the most advanced technological means. And—as we now know but refuse to believe— no nation with superweaponry at its disposal, and with a superidentity to lose, is above the temptation to exterminate (in occasional massacres or planned bombardments) what it considers to be an expendable species. All the more reason, then, now that we have become a species mortally dangerous to itself, to follow the idea of pseudospeciation underground, and to gain some insight into our very deep resistance to insights which dethrone our sense of centrality in the universe.

But here, as elsewhere, the worst in us is intimately related to the best, and the most atavistic to the renewal of mankind's search for a more universal identity. And even as we find what we would nowadays call a rationalized racism in the world-image of Jefferson's time, and a practical as well as intellectual racism in his own writings, it is more important to gain painful insights into our common evolutionary and developmental corruptability than an easy moral superiority over our dead heroes. The process of pseudospeciation which has blurred the borderlines between reality and illusion and set man against man in the name of commitments to the death has also produced those more universal civilizations and, with them, the networks of communication on which a wider human consciousness will depend.

In the light of all this we can now appreciate the shining newness of the American identity as it emerged against the background of the unbelief of the parental Old World. The faith in that newness which included the power to renew newness itself exists in all of us to this day even though we are only too aware of the fact that the revolutionary *homo novus* (such as the "natural aristocrat" who in Jefferson's own time was to defeat the "pseudo-aristoi" of the old regime) would eventually masquerade in a range of roles and stances quite at odds with the originator's vision. And yet, that revolution, that emergence of an identity then newer and wider than any preceding one, is still with us and not only because there will always be anniversaries to recall such beginnings. Much of the rest of the world, even where it tends to malign our crudities, smiles at our purist pretensions, and abhors our excesses in the use of mechanical power, still looks to America as one model, however tainted, of a historical miracle.

As I now proceed to offer something of an anatomy of a new identity and attempt to relate it to universal psychological needs, I must make use of the license provided with these lectures, and emphasize some of its roots in Jeffersonian thought. How these aspirations and images were, once a nation was born, ever more rapidly counterpointed by emerging divisions into a Northern and a Southern hemisphere, into agrarian and mercantile, conservative and populist power spheres, and how there emerged what John Adams called a "long catalogue of illustrious men," each of a distinct personality and idiosyncratic style—all that I must neglect.

And lest a new identity, now that it is fashionable to invent one's own, may seem grandiosely improvised, let me be didactic and postulate that any true identity is anchored in the confirmation of three aspects of reality. One is *factuality*, that is, a universe of facts, data, and techniques that can be verified with the observational methods and the work techniques of the time. Then, there is an inspiringly new way of experiencing history as unifying all facts, numbers and techniques into a *sense of reality* that has visionary qualities and yet energizes the participants in most concrete tasks. And, finally, there must be a new *actuality*, a new way of relating to each other, of activating and invigorating each other in the service of common goals. Maybe one should not hesitate to add a fourth condition which could be called luck or grace, and which in pragmatic America was to be called chance. Given chance, however, only these three together—factuality, reality, and actuality (and I will come back to all three)—combine to that sense of self-evident truth which Jefferson was so singularly able to put into words.

The most fundamental new fact was, of course, the expanse of territory, a virgin wilderness with undreamt of resources only waiting for agricultural enterprise and experimentation. "In Europe," Jefferson said, "the object is to make the most of their land, labor being abundant, here it is to make the most of our labor, land being abundant." But if a new identity also needs a new sense of reality, that, in turn, demands not only a freedom for a joint future but also a liberation from past obligations which could mortgage the present. The revolutionary leaders had to impress on the people that they had a right to abandon their loyalties as children (or, for that matter, stepchildren) of their mother countries and fatherlands—and, as you may know, these are words explicitly used and used with passion at the time. They had come, these immigrants, to "realize on this continent the very possibilities of Creation itself." This, in turn, called for a new relationship to the heavens. Rush could call Franklin "that man whose mind like a mirror has long reflected back upon the deity, a miniature picture of its own works." And Jefferson could say of David Rittenhouse, who had built a model of the universe, "He has not indeed made the world, but he has by imitation approached nearer its Maker than any man who has lived from the Creation to this day." This manner of speech, of course, has persisted to our time when their president, by transspace telephone, could tell the first Americans on the moon that their deed was the greatest moment since creation. . . .

And how about the Creator himself? He was called the Maker, or the Fabricator, and Jefferson also referred to him as the Preserver and the Regulator: the fact is, God himself was remade in the American image. He was no bungler, Jefferson assured his friends. He had made the world in one week, for, as Jefferson said (and I challenge you to find a more imperious statement) "as the hand of a Creator is to be called in, it may as well be called in at one stage of the process as another." Called in by whom, one wonders. Here, God's creation was seen by God's creature in the light of the creature's historical vision. And the universe, it appeared, was less lonely for it. As Thomas Paine put it, "The solitary idea of a solitary world rolling on in the immense ocean of space, gives place to the cheerful idea of a society of worlds so happily contrived as to administer, even by their motion, instruction to man."

Speaking of the Maker, I have always been fascinated by such Americanisms as the many uses of the word *make*. Ever since I was first told, having arrived in this country with eight hundred words of basic English and having settled down to work, "You've got it made," I have wondered over the fate of this word in basic American. And Jefferson did say that he hoped for an American language "so that its new character may separate it, in name as well as in power, from the mother tongue." At any rate, I invite you to think about this word *make* in its many forms, such as "to be on the make," "making it," or "to make out together." But, alas, also to "make like," for all such basic words have double meanings. "Happily contrived," said Paine. And come to think of it, the very word *fabricator* has a built-in ambiguity, such as fully emerged in the ideal of the new *man* who soon became the *new* man who forever made his deals with new ideals and new facts. Fortunately, however, the founders saw to it that this new factual world and this new concept of reality also inspired a new actuality in the form of the participation of all (certified) citizens in the life of the community and that of the communities in the hierarchies of the federated structure.

You may have noticed that I have sketched the outline of a space-time vision which I must now make explicit. Left *behind* in the *past*, there was a guilt disproven, a doom overcome, and, in fact, an election confirmed: Here the Bible obliged by offering an identification with the Israelites whom God had guided across another water to the promised land. *Ahead* in the *future*, there was a chance just waiting for the newly liberated man. Then there was an assured sanction from *above*, that sanction from way above which reflects (and reflects on) those who, before the very eyes of their constituents, emerged as the founding fathers. But, alas, the new identity, to define itself, also needs some people *below*, who must be kept in their place, confined, or even put away. For in order to live up to a new self, man always needs an otherness to represent at the bottom of the social scale that *negative identity* which each person and each group carries within it as the sum of all that it must not be. In a do-it-yourself identity such otherness would be characterized by an inability (also seemingly God given) to help *oneself*—or is it to *help* oneself? There were the slaves, doomed to help others. There were the sick and the mad who cannot help it. And then there are always the bad who could help it but won't.

But if, indeed, the very center of this world seems to be occupied by the ideal of the self-Made man, where is the place of woman? Oh, she is by his side as his helpmate; and it will call for a ruthless and indiscreet kind of history to determine where, in the division of functions, she joined those above him (for example, as motherly ideal and guardian of manners), those below him (in the domestic and sexual sphere), and those unfranchised in either state or church.

But let me now put aside this phenomenological and vastly simplified approach to the new identity until, in the second lecture, I can make it more dynamic by asking why individuals must live by such visions. I still owe you a brief discussion of another book.

The Perspective of the Mount

THE VIEW FROM Monticello, as contained in the *Notes on the State of Virginia*, was written, we said, at the lowest moment of Jefferson's career when the political survival of the continent, of Virginia, and of the author himself was at stake. I pointed to a few of the writer's identity elements visible in that work; we will summarize those in conclusion. But now to the review of the actions and sayings of Jesus—a review of a very different kind, which Jefferson undertook during the second half of his life, and, in fact, at the height of his career as a statesman. Because of the central prominence in it of the Sermon on the Mount, I will characterize this outlook as the Perspective of the Mount.

In 1801, Jefferson had become president with an overwhelming mandate from the people, though not without being exposed to such slanderous reportage as was to become typical for American campaigns but which could only deeply offend a man who, on the one hand, was so jealous of his public image, and yet so ready to disavow ambition and to withdraw to Monticello. Furthermore, the attacks on him concerned those most sensitive and central aspects of a man's life which Jefferson never aired in public: his personality, his (very) private life, and his religion. As he once put it, "I not only write nothing on religion, but rarely permit myself to speak of it, and never but in reasonable society." And so, during his first presidential campaign, he had to tolerate with silence the most sinister insinuations concerning the devastating consequences for the whole country of an atheist administration. And, indeed, all his life Jefferson avoided public Christian display and loud sectarian controversies and shunned any contrivance with clerical power struggles: "To the corruptions of Christianity I am, indeed, opposed; but not to the genuine precepts of Jesus himself. I am a Christian in the only sense in which he wished anyone to be; sincerely attached to his doctrines in preference to all others; ascribing to himself every *human* excellence; and believing that he never claimed any other."

Such a well-defined position, however, he could assume only on the basis of having surveyed the Scriptures with great care, if (again) a care which was guided by that pervasive sense of privileged selectivity which characterized his struggle for human integrity within his historical reality. And so, we must visualize an American president in the beginning of the nineteenth century spending evenings going over the New Testament, comparing its versions in Latin and Greek, French and English, and asking himself

line for line whether or not it spoke to him as the voice
of Jesus. These "authentic" parts he cut out and pasted together in a booklet which he called, "THE PHILOS-
OPHY OF JESUS OF NAZARETH extracted from the
account of his life and teachings as given by Matthew,
Mark, Luke and John. Being an abridgement of the New
Testament for the use of the Indians, unembarrassed with
matters of fact or faith beyond their comprehension."
Whatever the fate of his subtitle, it does seem to suggest
the writer's intent to present something of a native, an
American Gospel.

This, the historians tell us, refers to the compilation
which was completed in the years 1804–05, was shown
only to very few intimates, and then disappeared. It has
been reconstructed only recently and is said to be more
personal and more revealing than another compilation,
completed in the 1820s which, in turn, was called the *Life
and Morals of Jesus of Nazareth*, and came to public attention when it reached the National Museum in 1895.
For our purposes and for this lecture, this second compendium will and must do.

We owe ourselves a review of this effort, for it bespeaks
some awareness, on the part of an American president, of
the fact that one pole of any identity, in any historical
period, relates man to what is forever contemporary,
namely, eternity. And it permits us to sketch, if only in
broad strokes, this pole of identity, as it deals with the
awareness of death. We all dimly feel that our transient
historical identity is the only chance in all eternity to be
alive as somebody in a here and a now. We, therefore,
dread the possibility, of which we are most aware when
deeply young or very old, that at the end we may find

that we have lived the wrong life or not really lived at all. This dread seems incomparably greater than that of death itself, after a fulfilled life—awful as the sudden cessation of life always is. Therefore, human communities, whether they consist of a tribe set in a segment of nature, or of a national empire spanning the territory and the loyalties of a variety of peoples, must attempt to reinforce that sense of identity which promises a meaning for the cycle of life within a world view more real than the certainty of death. Paradoxically speaking, however, to share such a transient sense of being indestructible, all participants must accept a ritual code of mortality and immortality which (whether it promises a rebirth on earth or in heaven) includes the privilege and the duty, if need be, to die a heroic, or at any rate a shared death, while also being willing and eager to kill or help kill those on "the other side" who share (and live and kill and die for) another world view. The motto of this immortality, whether in combat or competition, can be said to be "kill and survive."

The men who inspire and accomplish such a world view we call great and we bestow a form of immortality on them: While they must die, as we must, their image, cast in metal, seems to survive indestructibly in the monuments of our town squares or in the very rock of Mount Rushmore.

But there is the other, the transcendent, effort at insuring salvation through a conscious acceptance of finiteness. It emphasizes nothingness instead of an insistance on somebodyness. It is "not of this world," and instead of a competition for the world's goods (including those securing the earthly identity) it seeks human brotherhood in self-denial. It courts death or, at any rate, self-denial as a step toward a more real and everlasting life. It prefers self-sacrifice to killing. And it visualizes the men and women who can make this aspect of existence convincing, not as great and immortal, but as saintly and as partaking of an eternal life. This way of identity is personified by the great religious leaders who in their own words represent the naked grandeur of the I that transcends all earthy identity in the name of Him who *is* I Am. The motto of this world view could be said to be "die and become."

History shows how these two forms of an immortal identity find their most elaborate communal expressions in empires and religions, which may remain infinitely antagonistic to each other or attempt reconciliation and collusion when priestly empires make political deals with the worldly ones. They may attempt to hasten with holy wars the salvation of the right-minded and the damnation of the rest. Reformations and revolutions upset such collaborations (until they form their own) and demand ideological commitment to one truth or the other. The main point of reviewing such grand schemes in such limited space is the suggestion that the readiness for both extremes, that is, for a defined identity in space and time and a transcendent one is given in all human beings. The biblical division of human duties allocated to Caesar and God makes the basic point that without a physical existence in an earthly regime there can be no defined self as a seat for an I in search of transcendence and no social order to support or to complement a religious domain. And it appears to have been the interplay between empires and world religions which in past history has worked toward a unified identity on earth.

Where the state succeeds in making the motto "kill and survive" so imperative that the voice of "die and become" is being silenced, religious men must oppose the state and, as some of our friends have done, put their bodies on the line. I have attempted to demonstrate with the means at my disposal Mahatma Gandhi's application of a nonviolent method to both national and spiritual liberation as the most systematic attempt in our times, significantly born on the other side of the globe, to a unification of action and faith in a self-aware, all-human identity. "God," he said, "appears to you only in action." Jefferson could have said that. And if Gandhi meant nonviolent action, I think one can find a strong temperamental trend—"peace is my passion" —toward solutions without violence in Jefferson's policies. In the meantime, it bespeaks Jefferson's, the nation builder's, classical sense of balance that he attempted to accommodate the postrevolutionary and the dominant religious identity to each other—for the sake of a new actuality with infinite possibilities.

It is this widest context—at the time underscored, no doubt, by a deep conflict between political triumph and the need for privacy—which gives significance to Jefferson's secret scholarly effort, even though radical religionists will characterize it more as pragmatic compromise with an economic ideal than as an existential commitment. As a friend of mine, great minister and activist, exclaimed when he found me studying this matter, "Oh, for that Jeffersonian faith: Christianity without sin!" A political cynic, in turn, may well suspect that Jefferson, when he undertook this work in the midst of violent political controversies, may have identified with Jesus as the one who drove the Hamiltonians out of the temple treasury. But let us see.

"I have," so Jefferson wrote in two letters, "made a wee

little book which I call the Philosophy of Jesus; it is a paridigm of his doctrines, made by cutting the texts out of the [New Testament] and arranging them on the pages of a blank book in a certain order of time or subject." And, "The result is an octavo of forty-six pages of pure and unsophisticated doctrines such as were professed and acted on by the *unlettered* Apostles, the Apostolic Fathers, and the Christians of the first century. The matter which is evidently his . . . is as easily distinguishable as diamonds in a dunghill."

Whatever latent motives, political or personal, will be found in the reconstructed early version, its base line, as it were, is the image which Jefferson had of the person of Jesus—an image of a very special son of the countryside: "His parentage was obscure, his condition poor; his education null; his natural endowments great; his life correct and innocent; he was meek, benevolent, patient, firm, disinterested, and of the sublimest eloquence."

My theological friends tell me that the selections of the later compendium in four languages stand up well under modern Bible research, which, in its own way, has entered the psychohistorical arena by asking what each particular Gospel writer, at what particular place and in what particular time, wrote for what audience, and what we may reconstruct of the writer's life history and personality before we undertake to see through all the haze of his self-expression and propagandistic effort who the man Jesus may have been and what he really said. Jefferson, we will not be surprised to hear, selected fully half of Matthew—the Gospel writer whom the scholars judge to be most "lucid, calm, tidy, and judicious." There are lesser portions of the others. The longest coherent section and the centerpiece of it all is the Sermon on the Mount, which sets the tone for the rest. The whole is above all a narrative, recording Jesus' travels and relating mainly facts—and not a single miracle! But it does report the parables which make the kingdom so agriculturally concrete. The kingdom of heaven is like "there was a landowner who planted a vineyard," or "like a mustard seed," or like "a treasure lying buried in the field." All this, it is clear, can be made to fit the agricultural destiny of the new world, where transcendence must emerge above all, from work, and where, therefore, actuality is faith, and faith, actuality.

If I, in my turn, may be permitted to be selective in my emphases, there is always the story which I would relate here even if Jefferson had not included it in his Gospel—as he luckily did: "And he came to Capernaum: and being in the house he asked them, 'What was it that ye disputed among yourselves by the way?'

"But they held their peace: for by the way they had disputed among themselves, who should be the greatest.

"And he sat down, and called the twelve, and saith unto them, 'If any man desire to be first, the same shall be last of all, and servant of all.'

"And he took a child, and set him in the midst of them: and when he had taken him in his arms, he said unto them,

" 'Whosoever shall receive one of such children in my name, receiveth me; and whosoever shall receive me, receiveth not me, but him that sent me.' " (Mark 9: 33–38)

A child, not a boy or a girl; a child in its sensory, sensual, and cognitive wholeness, not yet defined in sexual roles and not yet overdefined by economic ones. Such a one has that childlikeness, which to regain in the complexities of adult life, is the beginning of the kingdom. All else is history.

Jefferson's selection is, of course, as interesting in its omissions as it is in its commitments. The context of today's lecture permits me to point out, that what Jefferson discards as a "dunghill" is, in fact, the Gospel writers' pamphletistic attempt to convince their readers that Jesus is the product and the prophet of the coherent world vision prophesied by the books, and that he only confirmed, even as he renewed and restated, the Judaic world with its dooms and promises and, above all, its ethnic utopia. Jefferson obviously felt that this falsified rather than verified Jesus' most pervasive and most rebellious presence as well as the nature of the salvation he envisaged. And, indeed, it can be seen in many Gospel passages that Jesus was most diffident about the traditional, ceremonial, and professional roles which his followers wanted to foist on him, even as he was, in fact, diffident whenever the crowd wanted to define him in terms of his personal identity, his familial or geographic origin. At the end, so it seems he felt, only the final agony of the crucifixion could verify his transcendent identity. Jefferson excludes the story of the resurrection, but it is clear that he believed in the singular presence of Jesus among men.

If some critics miss all references to contrition in Jefferson's Gospel, it is true that the founding fathers did not go for what Thomas Paine called "theological inventions" which seduce man "to contemplate himself an outcast, at an immense distance from his Creator, so that he lost his sense for true religion." Faith in action demanded, as we saw, an intrinsic unity of divine and historical design.

But let me tell you what I find missing in Jefferson's selections. I miss, and I think not only out of professional pique, all references to Jesus' healing mission. Jesus' own diffidence in regard to his very success in the traditional healer's role explains well why Jefferson would want to omit all such references as an undue attempt to prove the legitimacy of Jesus by emphasizing his competence as a miracle doctor. And, we may add, Jefferson believed in the preventive powers of an active life more than he did in the healing arts, including the radical practices of his friend Dr. Rush. (Jefferson was once heard to say that when he saw two doctors in conversation, he scanned the sky for an approaching buzzard.) But I cannot forgive him for omitting the story which we need dearly so as to remain oriented in the history of healing concepts which, as I must show, change with any new identity. To me, the decisive therapeutic event in the Gospels appears in Luke 8: 48, and Mark 5: 25–35. It is the story of a woman who had lost not only blood for twelve years, but also all her money on physicians who had not helped her at all.

"When she had heard of Jesus, [the woman] came in the press behind, and touched his garment.

"For she said, 'If I may touch but his clothes, I shall be whole.'

"And straightway the fountain of her blood was dried up; and she felt in her body that she was healed of that plague.

"And Jesus, immediately knowing in himself that virtue had gone out of him, turned him about in the press, and said, 'Who touched my clothes?'

"And his disciples said unto him, 'Thou seest the multitude thronging thee, and sayest thou, Who touched me?'

"And he looked round about to see her that had done this thing.

"But the woman fearing and trembling, knowing what

was done in her, came and fell down before him, and told him all the truth.

"And he said unto her, 'Daughter, thy faith hath made thee whole; go in peace, and be whole of thy plague.'"

This story conveys themes which renew their urging presence in each age: There is the assumption of certain quantities lost and regained and with them a quality of wholeness. Jesus, too, notices that a quantity of virtue has passed from him to her—and this as she touched him, and not (according to the age-old technique) as his hand touched her. He felt her touch even in the general press that surrounded him, and this solely because her faith thus magnetically attracted some of his strength before he quite knew it. There could be no doubt, then, that it was her faith in his mission that had made her whole. This story is an exalted illustration of that dynamic element, that electric force which has always fascinated the healing professions, not the least in Jefferson's times when Rush as well as Franklin became acquainted with Mesmer's attempts to physicalize this quantity and its transfer, and again in our time when Freud assumed the misplacement of quantities of love and hate to be intrinsic to emotional disturbance, and transference essential for their cure.

Transformations in the over-all sense of identity (and it is obvious that the polarization of the Greco-Roman Empire and the Christian kingdom was such a transformation which eventually also influenced the new identity made in America) bring with them new approaches to sickness and madness. These are characterized by a greater internalization of the cause as well as the cure of the sickness ("your faith will make you whole") and thus by a greater ethical awareness on the parts of both healer and to-be-healed. How, in our time, insight thus joined faith as the therapeutic agent of wholeness, even as the theorizing about mysterious quantities continued—that, too, we will return to in the second lecture.

Protean President

LET ME, in conclusion, attempt to connect a few of the psychohistorical themes which have emerged in this lecture with the point of view I would represent before that imaginary academy convoked to integrate the data of Jefferson's life and personality.

Sooner or later, of course, Jefferson was to be called a *Protean* man. But this word is as elusive as the mythical figure whose name it bears, for as it means a man of many appearances, this meaning itself is hard to take hold of. It can and does denote a many-sided man of universal stature; a man of many gifts, competent in each; a man of many appearances, yet centered in a true identity. But it can also mean a man of many disguises; a man of chameleonlike adaptation to passing scenes; a man of essential elusiveness. According to our historical formula, however, any of these designations in a man of such stature, would have to be seen in relation to the new identity emerging in his time. As part of a self-made man a Protean personality would convey the ability to make many things of oneself, and this in a semideliberate and rebellious fashion. And, indeed, Jefferson, who always seems to anticipate with some lucky phrase whatever interpretation one comes to attach to him, once spoke of his early resolution "not to wear any other character than that of a farmer," which implies that he had a choice and chose an over-all appearance related to a specific work role. Such a role Jefferson could carry through with a special flair and not without coming into some poignant conflict with other roles. When, in the White House, he greeted the first British ambassador and his lady in worn-out slippers, he knew well what he meant to dramatize, considering his cold and formal reception, years before, at the Royal Court. The White House was the national homestead of free farmers.

Among the themes contributing to Jefferson's individual identity, in addition to natural aristocrat, I had occasion to mention several elements of intellectual and esthetic style: The amateur and the surveyor, the educator and the ideologue. Each of these elements could have been specialized in an occupational identity. Instead, they all pervaded a rich alternation of occupational roles: farmer and architect, statesman and scholar. But they were all guided by passionate choices of commitment (and here identity comes of age) to causes that needed to be taken care of competently. These, in turn, permitted Jefferson to combine contradictory modes of action—such as his grandiose expansionism as a statesman, who doubled the territory of the United States (and had it duly surveyed) during his administration, and the capacity and sometimes desperate need for seclusion in his private domain.

Even though Jefferson attests to no kinship with Goethe (whose language was one of the few truly foreign to him), my European education often makes me think of this man who was Jefferson's contemporary. He, too, integrated his many-sidedness in a carefully cultivated façade. Jefferson the amateur could, in fact, fall in love with façades such as the Roman temple in Nîmes ("No Madam . . . to fall in love . . . with a house . . is not without precedent in my history.") Maybe one must have been brought up in classical humanism to know that to say somebody loved façades, including his own, is no slur. This classical façade, no doubt, had much to do with the Greco-Roman stance cultivated by that other new, that Renaissance identity, which did so much to balance the Judaeo-Christian heritage of contrition. I would go further and say that Jefferson's tremendous correspondence, of which he himself kept such careful duplicates, constituted carefuly, craftsmanlike work on the desired historical appearance, even though he claimed to be fond of letter writing just because it so genuinely preserved "the warmth and presence of fact and feeling," and, in the life of some, "the only full and genuine journal of life." Jefferson's personality comes through exactly where he can combine, with supreme artistry, both façade and feeling, and ever again surprise others with a convincing informality well suited to his physical appearance of natural roughness and, yet, genuinely elegant stature. Where fact and feeling could not be surely fitted into the frame which he wished to immortalize, he destroyed even his correspondence, as he did that with his mother and his wife.

Such alternation of effusiveness and reserve makes, of course, any approach to a man's private personality hazardous. But we have no right to accuse him of the deliberate sabotage of our efforts which belong to such a different period. Yet, we remain curious as to what was behind the façade, and we want to know what such a façade cost a man in pained concerns about loss of face, in some deviousness of self-defense under attack, and in loneliness. He always held his head high, but, so it seems, only at the price of that occasional headache such as the one that befell him high up on the Natural Bridge. His outstanding symptom was incapacitating migraine, for weeks at a time. And he could fall to the ground and lie there as if lifeless in desperate mourning.

A façade exists to be seen, and in ascribing to an individual the intention or the need to maintain one, we must also ask who are his needy and obliging onlookers. And here, we may remember the history of monuments, not to speak of portraiture which, in Jefferson's time, combined a certain warmth of expression with a stance of reserve, uprightness, and farsightedness to which Jefferson's (and Washington's) body height and profiles lent themselves perfectly. Such façades arouse admiration to the point of canonization, for the exalted image of the human stature permits us to participate in the glorified uprightness which we, the vertical species on earth, need in order to hold our own heads high. But a façade also provides disbelief and suspicion, ranging all the way from the mild assertion that in some ways the hero seems to be human (meaning like us) to the pleasure of finding cracks in the great façade. All this can be transcended in some systematic fashion, only in the attempt to detect in the façade a truth which includes us, the beholders.

The analysis of how a person comes to choose such a public image, even though he himself may at times react diffidently to it, may begin with the call emanating from the historical situation. Jefferson's times demanded some self-aggrandizement in the service of the new, almost instant ancestral past which American history had to create. Besides the obligation to make his special gifts serve the new regime, and this with some grandeur (refreshingly counteracted in Franklin's humor), there must also be a special capacity to put such gifts to work.

In his study of Leonardo, Freud conceded that artistic gift as such escapes analysis. But so does any giftedness: For a gift there can be no itemized bill. The whole ecology of greatness, therefore, transcends many of the assumptions which clinical work has suggested regarding the inner economy of a person. They remain applicable, of course, to any leader's symptomatic behavior, which means either that he himself suffers from attacks beyond his control and comprehension, or, indeed, that he is judged by his intimates not to be quite himself. Where this leads to impulsive criminal acts transgressing what is expectable or tolerable in the ordinary collusions of any system of power, clinical considerations will, of course, help clarify events. Otherwise, the facile or biased use of psychiatric terms can only blind the observer to the historical issues at stake.

For example, it must be said that such a love of façade could not exist without a strong degree of that love of one's own image which we, technically, call narcissism. It was Narcissus who so fell in love with his own likeness as mirrored in a spring—a likeness reminding him of his dead twin sister—that he was unable to abandon it and perished by the side of the stream. The true—and potentially malignant—danger of narcissism, then, is a tendency in adolescence and beyond, to remain totally (and bisexually) absorbed in oneself instead of losing oneself in engagements with others. But it is obvious that a leader like Jefferson, whatever dangers of narcissism he may have harbored, as he sees himself mirrored in the imagery of a present and vital people, answers their call for leadership artfully and competently. And he was no show off: Not even in the defense of his eloquent authorship of the Declaration of Independence was he able to engage in oratory; while in his presidency, from the day of his inauguration he toned down public ceremony and private protocol, and this quite in contrast to the regal ceremonialism introduced by Washington.

A word about the child in the man. When I read to you some of Jefferson's descriptions of nature (and we have now added his love of beautiful buildings), you no doubt sensed in him a deep nostalgia which seems to have been lifelong—was it for that mysterious mother about whom, partially because he kept her from us, we as yet know so little? But how can one begin to analyze such a trend as unconscious in a man who could say of himself, when he finally retired to Monticello, "I fold myself into the arms of retirement"?

In rebuilding Monticello beyond all need (and he confessed to any true designer's delight in "putting up, and pulling down") he crowned the building with an octagonal dome, thus adding an equally dominant maternal element to the strong façade. He had once been "violently smitten" when beholding what is now the Palais de la Légion d'Honneur in Paris. But the Monticello dome is said to have been inspired by that of the Hall aux Bleds where he had first met a lady whom we will introduce presently. All one can say of this whole trend of nostalgia, then, is that while it endangered his composure at times, his ethos of self-made masculinity permitted and enabled him to plan his own maternal shrine, and to "fold himself into its arms." Retired, he spent his last years designing, founding, and caring for the University of Virginia, providing for future generations a cupola symbolizing an Alma Mater, and embracing "the human mind in this hemisphere." Let us not forget, then, to add *designer* to the essential elements of his identity.

All this was many years after Jefferson's married life had come to an abrupt end. Shortly after he had written the *Notes on the State of Virginia*, and before he turned forty, his wife died. He later said, "My history . . . would have been as happy a one as I could have asked could the objects of my affection have been immortal. But all the favors of fortune have been embittered by domestic losses. Of six children I have lost four, and finally their mother." In fact, only Martha, the oldest, survived him, being, while she was young, mothered by him as much as fathered, and later a maternal companion to him as much as a daughter.

The question of this widower's love life has haunted biographic imagination. It moves into the center of interpretation in our time when a man's sexuality has been recognized (from Nietzsche on) as prototypical for his personal style, not to speak of Freudian "libidinal economy" or Kinseyan "outlets." We do not easily give it credence, as Freud himself did, that special powers of sublimation may be assumed to exist in persons of such passionate devotion and minute service to public causes. At any rate, over the years, only two women have been mentioned as possible companions. One is Maria Cosway, an English woman whom he loved and lost while in Paris. His love for her is freely proclaimed in some now famous letters. When these were published as late as 1945, the reviewer in the *New York Times* remarked with a biographer's jealousy that they were "worthy of a better subject." But that graceful and vivacious, if undoubtedly somewhat flighty, woman (she, too, an Anglo-Saxon at home in Mediterranean culture), may have represented for him, as Carl Binger suggests, a Jungian "Anima" that is something of a female counterpart—a twin, indeed—whose presence evoked both a sense of wholeness and a rare quality of interplay. I will come back to the tragicomic end of this affair in the second lecture.

And, then, there is Jefferson's alleged liaison in later years, back on the plantation, with a much younger mulatto woman who is said to have borne him several children. The available data oscillate between conveying something that seems possible to something even probable. But here, too, an essential matter to be settled first is the attitude of the biographers. The term *African Venus* has attached itself to this woman, although she was only one-quarter black, and, in fact, the half-sister (sharing the same father) of Jefferson's much bemourned wife. Jefferson's possible fathering of her children is refuted as an act of unthinkable miscegenation, although these children would have been only one-eighth black and were, as we know from Jefferson's own *Farm Book*, permitted to disappear when they reached maturity, in order to pass into the general population. Here

there arise questions of value, tact, and tolerance which
(in my imaginary academy) only a consortium of women
and men could approach psychohistorically. For what,
one must ask at last, would these Southern ladies, and
domestic slaves have known and felt about their being rela-
tives? And what would it have meant for Jefferson whose
only son died unnamed, at the age of three weeks, to send
into safe oblivion a mulatto son who, in fact, is said to have
looked very much like him? These and many more questions will have to be accommodated before this liaison, if
factual, also can become real—for us. Whatever biographers will conclude in regard to such intimate matters, and,
no doubt, many incidences and utterances will be shown
to be indicative of regressive trends, Jefferson was a man
of rare adult stature, caring intensely and competent to
take care of what he undertook—publicly and privately.
If he deserves the name founding father, he certainly de-
served that of father. His lapses and defeats, too, must be
seen in this larger context of a mature consummation of
the cycle of life.

As for the pervasive Protean quality—does this not make
him intensely American and both prototypical and unique
among the leaders of his time? It is hard to believe today—
for we believe we started it in our time—how conscious
these early Americans were of the job of developing an
American character out of the regional and generational
polarities and contradictions of a nation of immigrants and
migrants. And *character* here, again, meant many things:
the clear differentiation of a new identity transcending and
yet aware of its links to those left behind in the mother
countries; a new typology embodying a cast of clearly
drawn, and often overdrawn, characters depicted in highly

self-conscious formative novels; and the moral strength demanded of self-made men, not to become the forever adjustable puppets of new conditions and improvised mores. For the overwhelming quantitative changes (there were ten million Americans by the time of Jefferson's death) soon began to defy the founders' design. Just because of this once-in-history chance for self-made newness, this country has experienced greater expansiveness and yet also deeper anguish than have other countries; and few nations have seen their ideals and their youth divided, as has this country in the recurring divisions of a national identity. Was the happiness guaranteed in the Declaration that of wealth and of technological power or that of an all-human identity such as resides primarily in the free person? Is there any other country which continues to ask itself not only "What will we produce and sell next?" but ever-again "Who are we anyway?" which may well explain this country's hospitality to such concepts as the identity crisis which, for better or for worse, now seem almost native to it.

The monumental achievement of Jeffersonian biography, then, as it stands and as it is still developing, can find some complement in psychohistorical approaches. The emotional hazards of doing biographical and historical work have become conscious to every Jefferson scholar. Jefferson's image does not settle for less. If such work awakens new aspirations in history writing, it also suggests a certain resignation concerning that definitive biography or history that is forever about to be written. Maybe all that can be hoped for is a conscious and disciplined assessment of the true relativity of the best of historical data, and of our own lives as observers.

II.

The Inheritors:
Modern Insight and Foresight

The "Living Generation" and Other Quotations

In the first lecture I concentrated on Jefferson as one of the founding personalities in the emergence of a new identity. Today we will have to let go of the great man and face a few questions concerning us, the inheritors. Within the limit of one lecture we must inquire what it is in each of us that seems to need a sense of newness in every epoch of history, in every new stage of our lives, and, in fact, every morning as we start the day? This, in turn, may help us to grasp, in psychological terms, some of the singular significance of the phenomenon of the United States.

Those of us who have been occupied with biography, as readers or as writers, know that to leave a great man and to face ourselves again, can give us something of a chill. But there are always quotations—that echo of forever memorable sentences which assure the great man's im-

mortality, and ours. For example, as we turn from Jeffersonian action to certain psychological insights of our day,
this is how Jefferson sends us on the way: "The times in
which I have lived, and the scene in which I have been
engaged, have required me to keep the mind too much in
action to have leisure to study minutely its laws of action."

But what laws of the mind's action would Jefferson have
been able to study? I must admit it, his naturalist inclinations
might have led him into a psychology very different from
the one I represent. The psychology he admired most was
that of the French physiologist Pierre Cabanis, to whose
lectures he had listened in Paris with fascination. As he
wrote to Adams, Cabanis had demonstrated with brain
surgery on animals that "the anatomical structure of certain portions of the human frame" proved them to be
"capable of receiving from the creator the faculty of
thinking." 'Materialist psychiatry,' his approach has been
called. And if this brings to mind the kind of behaviorist
psychology, based on the study of pigeons and rats, which
has culminated in this country and in our day in the
utopia of an environment so perfectly designed that lifelong conditioning would replace moral conflict, Dr. Benjamin Rush, Jefferson's friend and our ancestor in American psychiatry, anticipated such a view. He was convinced
that the very fall in paradise was meant to condition man
for faith in labor. God, far from imposing a curse on man,
merely "rendered . . . the salutary stimulus necessary . . .
in the more active form of labor," and thus, obviously, also
laid the foundation for the American work ethos, the surest
antidote against primal guilt. More pharmacologically (and
Rush helped to found this branch of medicine, too) Moses
ground the golden calf into a powder which he made the

idolators drink. Since this medicine was "bitter and nauseating in the highest degree . . . an inclination to idolatry [henceforth] could not be felt without being associated with the remembrance of this disagreeable mixture, and of course being rejected, with equal abhorrence."

Today, two hundred years of "freedom and dignity" later, B. F. Skinner claims that "a culture is very much like the experimental space used in the analysis of behavior. . . . A child is born into a culture as an organism is placed in an experimental space." And he is convinced that we could develop a "technology of behavior" which minimizes the possibility of "aversive" consequences and maximizes the achievements we desire. It would be fascinating to compare the original American world view which we discussed in the first lecture with Skinner's cosmology, in which the "environment" takes over the function of "the inner gatekeeper," namely conscience.

But if we ask who will then be the top gatekeeper in a perfectly planned world, the Jeffersonians, one remembers, managed to be naturalists and deists, and to them it was God who was the great director of the cosmic laboratory designed to condition man in his very image. Who would be Skinner's nomination for that top job?

I need not tell you how far apart is Skinner's world and that of psychoanalysis; he makes that clear enough. And yet the two approaches respectfully converge in one concern which they, in turn, share with the Jeffersonians. It is the concern of replacing, each according to its own method, that deadly combination of the best and the worst in man which his conscience has turned out to be, whether he must punish himself or others in order to have a good conscience or, at least, to make a guilty one bearable. "Punished behavior," Skinner confirms, "is likely to reappear after the punitive contingencies are withdrawn." But Skinner denies us any suggestion of a political structure of that planned environment in which shame, guilt, and sin will be abolished because incentive to do what causes them will be gone. And so we can only shudder at the implications of a rationale such as this: "We try to design such a world for those who cannot solve the problem of punishment for themselves, such as babies, retardates, or psychotics, and if it could be done for everyone, much time and energy would be saved." We shudder because we know only too well what kind of political mind would be only too willing to help out in administering this clinical world laboratory.

Let me, then, take recourse to some other quotations which might guide us to matters closer to my thinking, concerned as it is with the ontogeny of conscience in the generational succession of life cycles.

* * *

Let me present a few excerpts from Jefferson's correspondence with his daughter, and remind you of one more period in his life, a veritable crisis of the middle years, midway between his Virginia governorship and his presidency. You may remember that the low point of his political career (when he wrote the *Notes on the State of Virginia*) was followed by the deepest personal sorrow, the death of his wife. Having undergone an extraordinary period of mourning, he had ceased to resist the call of national office, especially since it revived an old dream—to live in Paris. There (now in his mid-forties and minister to France), he had fallen in love with a younger Englishwoman—married, as were all his women friends. She was an artist who seems to have freed in him much of his lighter side, as he was to attest somewhat mournfully in "The Head and the Heart," that most famous love letter known to have been written by a future president of the United States—so far. I promised to report to you the end of this affair. On one of his last walks with the lady in a Paris park, Jefferson must, as we would say in basic American, have jumped the traces, for he fell and broke his right wrist, one of those joints the strategic function of which is fully realized only when it is put out of commission; and for Jefferson it was the wrist that moved the bow of his beloved violin, and that guided the pen with which he wrote his letters. He himself, as usual, not only felt the deeper meaning in this event but could express it in one or two sentences: "How the right hand became disabled would be a long story for the left to tell. It was by one of those follies from which good cannot come, but ill may," he wrote to a young friend at the time.

One could, and others rightfully will, make much of this event and this confession. At any rate, a few weeks of unparalleled emotional freedom had ended in a fall and a permanent injury.

Jefferson went to take the cure in Southern France where he received a letter from his daughter, Martha, now in her middle teens, who had joined him in France to go to school near Paris. She wrote, "Titus Livius puts me out of my wits. I cannot read a word by myself, and I read of it very seldom with my master; however, I hope I shall soon be able to take it up again."

Anyone who knows the stern and schoolmasterly tone of some of Jefferson's letters to his young daughters realizes that this passage was prime provocation. And it worked. He answered, "I do not like your saying that you are unable to read the ancient print of your Livy, but with the aid of your master. We are always equal to what we undertake with resolution." And he warns her, "If at any moment, my dear, you catch yourself in idleness, start from it as you would from the precipice of a gulph" for "idleness begets ennui, ennui, the hypochondria, and that a diseased body." This, I must admit, is a formula for health which my training has denied me. (And yet it seems to be alive, for the other day a New York taxi driver, zigzagging down Fifth Avenue at the rush hour, warned me, "Don't let it worry you. It would make you sick.") Jefferson reinforces his clinical threats with patriotic admonition: "It is part of the American character to consider nothing as desperate; to surmount every difficulty by resolution and contrivance. Remote from all other aid, we are obliged to invent and to execute; to find means within ourselves and not to lean on others." And he concludes, "No laborious person was yet hysterical." This veritable syndrome of threats—idleness and ennui, hypochondria and disease, un-Americanism and hysteria—permits me to remind you of the negative identity, that necessary counterpart of any positive one. It is really as if (as Kai Erikson suggests in his book, *Wayward Puritans*) any new identity harbored a line-up of deviancies which define the boundaries (here marked by a "precipice" and a "gulph") of the officially sanctioned character.

Equally memorable is the adolescent (and very American) daughter's undaunted and pointed answer, which exposes the father's moralistic stance: "I hope your wrist is better and I am inclined to think that your voyage is rather for your pleasure than for your health. I hope, however, it will answer both purposes. . . . I shall take up my Livy, as you desire it. I shall begin it again, as I have lost the thread of the history. As for the hysterics, you may be quiet on that head, as I am not lazy enough to fear them." That his daughter could thus talk back to him, and teasingly so, bespeaks Jefferson's own personal balance between a strong morality and a rebellious spirit—a combination probably fostered in him by *his* father. This daughter, Martha, as we recounted, was to be the only one of his children to survive him and maintain throughout his later life a fascinating role as womanly companion, even while she was bearing thirteen children to her husband.

If Thomas Jefferson here sounds somewhat punitive toward a daughter who seems to be well able to take it, we cannot even begin to recount how slowly in his time cruel treatment of children became transformed into mere "psychological warfare". Normal man, so proud and yet so vulnerable in his resolution and contrivance seems to feel righteously justified in teaching a lesson to those who are helpless, because they are dependent, or those who he feels could help it, but are too weak in character.

Physical binding, flogging, and cold water treatments only gradually gave way to moral instruction. And as to the other deviants included in the negative identity, for example, people gone mad, they were chained and kept in dark and narrow places, their scalps were shaved and blistered, their bodies bled and purged. Patrick Henry, the great orator, when at home, had to feed his raving wife who was chained in the cellar. Rush (whose son, himself a doctor, became criminally and hopelessly insane) was one of the first to recognize the emotional origins of some sickness and of most madness, and to advocate occupational therapy as well as hygiene and kindness, even for psychotics. Yet, while madness could be caused by moral factors, the result remained physical, and Dr. Rush was a fanatic bloodletter. As for criminals, Jefferson himself, as a young lawyer and lawgiver, compiled a list of amputatory punishments of the most concrete eye-for-an-eye logic. This list, too, is contained, albeit inconspicuously, in the *Notes on the State of Virginia.* He was appalled about this later; and it must be said that when he had undertaken this assignment for a legislative committee he had attempted to limit the application of capital punishment by making circumscribed mutilation seem logical and just.

The point to be made here, is that the treatment of those who deviate from the path of adult normality, is somehow related to the way each individual treats threatening deviations in himself: It is as if the configurations of outer suppression are related to those of inner repression. Thus, if we make children stand in a corner or stay in some enclosure, if we incarcerate (even suspected) delinquents in narrow or overcrowded cells, or, as it were excarcerate dissenters beyond our borders and excommunicate and ban nonbelievers, the logic, not to speak of the benefit of such arrangement is certainly doubtful—but not so our satisfaction in having done to the transgressors what they had coming to them. There were, no doubt, practical reasons for confining orphans as well as psychotics, syphilitics, and destitutes in one jail-like building as was still done in Jefferson's time. But one may get an inkling from his letter how the positive identity must ever fortify itself by drawing the line against undesirables, even as it must mark itself off against those negative potentials which each man must confine and repress, deny and expel, brand and torture, within himself.

Yet Jefferson, the educator, was aware of the fact (and this way ahead of his time and especially of his own social setting) that cruelly punitive and vindictive behavior on the part of adults was dangerous for children not only when vented against them but also when done to others and witnessed by them. Here, I will end my introductory quotations by repeating once more a memorable passage which we must have before us in this lecture, too: "If a parent could find no motive either in his philanthropy or his self-love, for restraining the intemperance of passion towards his slave, it should always be a sufficient one that his child is present. . . . The parent storms, the child looks on, catches the lineaments of wrath, puts on the same airs in the circle of smaller slaves, gives a loose to his worst of passions, and thus nursed, educated, and daily exercised in tyranny, cannot but be stamped by it with odious peculiarities. The man must be a prodigy who can retain his manners and morals undepraved by such circumstances."

Philanthropy here means more than doing good, self-love more than pride, the children's presence more than an embarrassing circumstance. Together, they represent the informed love of humanity—in others, in himself, and in his children—which alone can help man to overcome his worst passion: The punitiveness by which he destroys not only those whom he beats into submission, but also takes risks with his own chance of truly respecting himself. Today, such passion is well disguised (so some adults think) when expressed in mechanized punitiveness on a large and more impersonal scale in far away countries against those not of our kind. Yet, it is literally brought home to our children by the media, and one wonders whether it does not threaten a whole generation with what Jefferson had in mind when he used the words "odious peculiarities."

All of this brings us to Jefferson's most famous saying which is, in fact, quoted on the invitation to these lectures: "The earth belongs always to the living." This he underscored by adding; "The dead have neither powers nor rights over it." Jefferson originally meant by this the legal mortgaging of the next generation by the attachment of the father's debts on the real estate inherited by the son. He himself had suffered under such a loaded inheritance from his father-in-law. But soon, and, of course, quite in the spirit of the revolution, this saying was applied to the whole problem of laws which force future generations to abide by a legal logic not affirmed by their own experience, and thus by the "sovereignty of the living generation." Merrill Peterson has called this "at once the most original and the most radical of Jefferson's political ideas." And, indeed, Jefferson as a lawgiver was forever preoccupied with matters of the generations, with the right to education and with freedom of (informed) conscience. And it was, indeed, Jefferson who once said (and some of the younger ones among you have asked me to confirm that he said it), "God forbid that we should ever be twenty years without . . . a rebellion." Why twenty years? Did he, maybe, refer not only to history but also to the life cycle: God forbid anybody should be twenty years old without having rebelled? At any rate, twenty years is about the span of human development needed for the individual to acquire a sense of identity firm and informed enough to act: which requires enough experience to acknowledge the power of facts and the facts of power; enough practical idealism to attach infantile ideals to live persons and issues; and enough rebellious commitment to the future to leave behind some of the internalized debt of infantile guilt.

Jefferson's saying, like all great sayings, remains alive as man's experience expands. Where his "earth" meant at first the earth under our feet, bounded by property lines in a new land still defining its over-all boundaries, it has come to mean to us the globe inhabited by one mankind, if not a spaceship in the perspective of outer space. If inheritance meant material enrichment or indebtedness transferred to the inheritors from those who wanted to leave something behind to perpetuate their name, today we are aware of the way in which older generations mortgage the inner ground of living. We know that each new generation carries within it a conscience weighted down with debts of guilt as well as of compliance implanted in the helplessness of childhood. But we also know that the resulting cruelty of man to man and of man to himself is grounded in the course of evolution and the history of civilization. To chart the tragic closeness of the best and the worst in man today also means to relate the fatal affinity of humanity's triumphs to its inhuman self-negation. But instead of preaching the loftier aspects conveyed by our string of quotations, let me attempt to bring out their import for human development. For, to summarize this introduction, the basic declaration that all men are created equal can mean to us only that all individuals are born with some capacity to develop and that each child born has a right to expect a chance to develop such potential. And to be born, mind you, from here on, means to be either chosen to be born or, alas, to have been born by default. In either case, it must mean the right to live in a community which chooses to guarantee, because it knows it lives by, the fullest development of each of its members.

The Old New Identity

I⊤ WILL BE clear by now that we cannot separate life history from history; and so, to relate at least one basic theme in human development to historical vision, I must briefly remind you of the universal dimensions of that New World image which provided the setting in space and time for the new identity.

World views, whether mythical or historical, have always had it both ways: They were projections of a people's earthly condition on the universe and a reprojection of such cosmic elaboration on man—so that a king could point to God and claim that God pointed right back at him, confirming that they were of one intention, one origin. Cosmogony coincided with the origin of the people—and the crown. But I wonder whether there has ever been a world view directed toward the future as was the

American dream which anticipated what new things were going to be done on a new continent, what new character of man and woman was going to emerge here, what news was going to be made.

In introducing all this with a "View from Monticello" I have, of course, spotlighted unduly what was pronounced by Jefferson himself and by orators and philosophers in correspondence with him. Obviously, the over-all world view emerged in local variations over the whole rapidly expanding land and was both floridly pronounced and eagerly assented to by the common man, as the American language attests. It came to be counterpointed in a variety of native types and homegrown slogans in which unlimited progress soon came to usurp the place of such early ideals as Jefferson's natural aristocracy. The antagonism between the Southern Athens and the Northern Sparta which had been so grandiosely bridged (with significant interruption) in the correspondence of Jefferson and Adams, already in their lifetime deepened to the point of no return, except by civil strife. But by then a complex American world view had taken hold, of which I can summarize only the simplest dimensions or, if you wish, the minimum requirements for each individual involved, leader or led. For it must be clear—and clearer today than ever—that in the vast complexity of political life, often most basic images and emotions of utmost simplicity carry the day. And so I consider it my task today, within the limits of this second lecture, to indicate what the psychological fascination of the American dream was and still is—for better, we hope, as for worse, we fear.

In the center of that world image, so I have said, was a new man, self-made in an America dedicated to natural labor, within naturally chosen institutions, guaranteeing a reciprocation of rights. As he was looking around and ahead, this new man saw a virgin continent as well as unlimited opportunities and raw materials which promised him that he would realize a new chapter, if not the main chapter, in creation. A limitless future, then, seemed confirmed, and with it a state of having arrived at a destination, rather than having abandoned, or, indeed, having been forced to leave a past abode. This prospect of a joint and blessed future, we said, was of special importance for a population that had come for a variety of temperamental and personal reasons and was impelled by a variety of political and religious pressures. It put an ideal of future performance (and a divine command performance at that) ahead of whatever fear or guilt or remorse may have come along in the immigrant's mental baggage. For immigrants in accepting a new identity (or a new version of their old one) at the price of instant identification and intense work, must leave behind not only old countries but also unlived futures, and not only enemies to be disavowed but also friends to be left behind—maybe to perish. What right, then, does the immigrant have to usurp a new identity? "Welcome" was still the official greeting to new arrivals in my day.

To the early American, who by a war barely won, had put behind him the old mother countries and the old fatherlands, with their deep inner hold on their erstwhile children and stepchildren, the past became a curse averted, a doom left behind. Nothing less was at stake than the conviction that the fate of immigration amounted—if not in the first generation, then in a subsequent one—to an elect state for generations to come, sanctioned from above in the name of God, of fate, and of history. And, indeed, the American had his Maker, his Creator, his Fabricator, who in the process was himself remade in the image of a rather excellent craftsman only too glad to favor his own type on earth. The founding fathers served as his mediators. Their statues would be cast in metal and erected in the town squares, their posture forever upright and their far-reaching gaze undaunted by weather or blaring parades, by noisy traffic or omnipresent pigeons. But, alas, as we also emphasized, man always needs somebody who is below him, who will be kept in place, and on whom can be projected all that is felt to be weak, low, and dangerous in oneself. If Americans had not had the Indians and the blacks—who far from having conquered their land could not defend it, or who, far from having wanted to come here had been forced to—the new Americans would have had to invent somebody else in their place.

So far the only system visible in such a sketch of a world view would seem to be a kind of weather vane pointing straight up to heaven and being grounded in a firm and yet elevated place where it maintains a sameness of fixed directions combined with a readiness to adjust to expectable change. For the moment, I suggest you keep such an image in mind. But lest such a world view seem oversimplified, and the corresponding identity a stance easy to contrive and to impersonate (for this is what identity has come to mean to all too many today), let me remind you also that I related the viability of such newness to historical reality, and thus first of all to the body of facts then known to observation and verifiable in technical, political, and military action. I separated from such *factuality* that sense of *reality* which lends coherence to the old as well as the new facts and gives to a sizable number of participants a heightened sense of being involved in events of significance. And finally I referred to *actuality* as that mutual activation which gives a special energy to economic, political, and personal activity. Only this threefold anchoring of a given world image in facts and figures cognitively perceived and logically arranged, in experiences emotionally confirmed, and in a social life cooperatively affirmed, will provide a reality that seems self-evident.

In America, however, more than anywhere in world history, such truth was and remained associated with newness forever renewed. This requires a stance which can be genuinely invigorating and yet, as happens to most revolutionary stances, can become obsessive—in this case, a sensational newness for its own sake. Or is it for its own sake, really? Could it not be that newness (new frontiers, new deals) also must provide a kind of self-amnesty for past failures in performance and in spirit? By the way of counterpoint, however, there is in this country also a persistent demand for a rebirth of authenticity, traditional or radical. No wonder that this struggle for a new identity, rewarded as it was by unheard of affluence, has not only attracted waves of immigrants to this country, but has also seductively and vigorously influenced new identities emerging in the rest of the world. Directly or indirectly, the American revolution has had an enduring hold on the imagination of peoples, even of those who have undergone radically different revolutions or evolutionary developments of their own.

But before I attempt to ground the dimensions of such a world view in at least one aspect of individual development, I must answer a just reservation: How can we possibly accept the world view of Jeffersonian times as an illustration valid for other times, not to speak of the present? Did Jefferson not believe that the ideal community was six miles in diameter with easy walking time to the periphery and back—and not riding time, mind you, for even horseback riding, according to him, was ruining the stamina of the legs man is born to stand and move on? He did. And did he not at one time wish that all manufacturing could remain in Europe, so that America might remain the country of agriculture and crafts? Yes, he did. I do not need to detail in comparison our gigantic urbanization and industrialization. While I was rereading the *Notes on the State of Virginia* and recalling the Blue Hill Mountains, gateway to an as yet unknown West, I was living on a peninsular hill in the Bay of San Francisco. From where I sat, I could see both the Golden Gate Bridge, portal to the Pacific, and the San Francisco Bay Bridge which leads inland toward the Continental Divide. Tens of thousands of vehicles cross these bridges every day; and hundreds of thousands of people live on the hills which they connect. At that time, as the moon hung over this panorama, Americans were up there and you could see them hopping weightlessly on your television screen.

Jefferson's friend Rittenhouse advocated that we should always include in our world view what we can see with macroscope and microscope. A comparative suggestion today would include instruments which are said to be close to reaching the end of space and fathoming the origins of life. That much for the facts. Reality? How can we really grasp, in one lifetime—to speak only of what America has wrought—Hiroshima, the moon landings, or, for that matter, our moral malaise at the height of our mechanized power of destruction? And, as for actuality, how few of us can feel sufficiently in touch with a sufficiently significant number of human beings to be activated by and to activate them, insulated as so many of us are in compartments within the gigantic networks of long-range mobility, of industrial complexes, and telecommunication?

The severe consequences of all this for the psychological ecology of man are being widely recognized and studied. But it is clear that no superorganizational remedies can work without the emergence of a new measure of man—which always means the awareness of a new center dynamically related to a fathomable periphery. That periphery is now marked by what man and machine can do and reach together without outreaching the industrious, inventive, and adaptive center—man himself. We must, therefore, take seriously such phenomena as a spontaneous new search for centeredness arising in this country. There is no doubt that cities, expanding skyward as outward, must and will be planned sooner or later around defined areas permitting communities to remain in touch and to meet face to face, no matter what wider and widest information will be conveyed to all by the media. And there is much talk, often mystifying and yet often quite simply felt, of what it might mean to be a human being—a term as vague and abused and yet to many as self-evident as Jefferson's "living generation." What is at stake here is not (or not primarily) a romantic return to a Walden between the high-rises. Rather, the measure of man is being recognized as centering in the development of the individual, and that always combines what the body can live by, what the mind can grasp, and what the person can integrate. For the basic fact that will always keep and bring us all closer together is the nakedness and helplessness of the newborn human child. Whether born in a high-rise hospital or in a farmhouse, in a geodesic dome or in the ghetto, born into a nuclear family or into a communal one, whether unbidden or joyously planned—once the newborn is here and is to survive at all, there must be a certain well-delineated environment of care adapted to the stages of human growth. And with each child will be born again not only all the capacity of the human brain's expansive mastery of yet inconceivable technical worlds but also certain fundamental trends emerging in circumscribed stages of development —trends to which evolution grants only an infinitesimally slow change. While man's inventions, self-conceptions, and aspirations may make radical leaps, other (more unconscious) parts of him change extremely slowly—I have referred to his conscience—and through stages which determine the final capacity to endure in the three spheres of reality which I outlined. It is for this reason that insights initiated by psychoanalytic exploration must continue to encompass the fundamental strengths and the lasting weaknesses which remain the basis of human motivation throughout life. To put it bluntly, what we must vigilantly pursue is the relationship of man's deals with his archaic inner life (his ego defenses, as they are called in my trade) and those political deals which mark the system of privileges and duties in his expanding world.

If we speak, for example, of an American dream, a collective dream of perpetual newness, is this just a manner of speaking, or is such a Dream with a capital D related to our individual nightly dreams? For we do spend a goodly portion of the time allotted to us lying down to sleep, which means not only to recover from the previous day's expenditure of energy and to awake recharged, but also to dream. And this, as we now know, means to return to se-lected portions of our personal and (some say) archaic past, in order to review (we see a dream) some images symbolic of some doubts aroused the day before and evoc-ative of the past. Awakening, we reorient ourselves, and this not only in regard to where we are, and with whom, but also who we are: And everyone (in very high places and in some low ones) knows the astonishment of meeting oneself in the mirror, as Mr., Mrs., or Ms. Such-and-such, defined, cornered, and yet strangely ready to face the day, and to get on with whatever labor and calling we live by. Here the collective vision counts as a background, for it helps us to slip not only into the clothes which mark our kind and our role, but also into the appropriate style of be-havior and into that heightened actuality which will—if it will—sustain us through the day.

From the Ground Up

THE THEMES of our nighttime horizontality and daytime verticality lead to a topic so elementary that I hesitate to present it in this august hall. I know that, sooner or later, I must come to contemporary issues. And yet, if in the first lecture I claimed contemporary status for eternity, I must now do so for evolution. When I sketched the space-time structure of one of those world views which have served as the ideological setting for man's political identity, I promised to come to the question of what such structures do for each individual involved. To answer this, I must begin with the simple fact that man, in evolution, turned into a creature who stood up and walked upright, and that every child will learn to stand on his own two feet. The anthropologist Weston La Barre once said, "Man stands alone, because man alone stands." We could add that because each of us stands alone, we must all stand together. One could say many more and much more complex things about the meeting points of psychology and political science; but, I submit, we must start here—from the ground up.

We all know, of course, the story of Oedipus, the usurper. But let us recall what the riddle was that the sphinx asked him to guess: "What walks on four feet in the morning, in midday on two, and on three in the evening?" Simple enough; and yet deeply personal, for Oedipus means "he with the swollen foot," a name signifying some stigmata in the lower extremities. The infant Oedipus' ankles had been pierced and tied with a thong before he was given away to be exposed on a mountain. Thus, one might say, the identity of the future riddle-solver and usurper of his father's throne and his mother's bed bore the curse of weak underpinnings. Oedipus' familial and public fate is the theme most fully explored by psychoanalysis. But while Freud, in the context of his libido theory did pay some earnest attention to the evolutionary significance of man's upright position (it exposes the male genitals and, we may add, the female breasts, prominent and permanent as in no other species), psychoanalysis has, I feel, not quite taken care of the singular importance of verticality for the human ego. Could it be that it has failed to do so because in its clinical laboratory the subject under observation is, in fact, asked to observe a horizontal position? And yet, the very wording of the riddle points not only to the phylogenetic given of man's verticality—inseparable from his stereoscopic vision and the miraculous freedom and refinement of his hands—it emphasizes the stage-by-stage aspect of the matter, the fatefully long span of infancy and the slow transition from supine dependence on the motherly person to an upright autonomy from her, which together spells both intense incestuous fixation—and hubris. And both will adhere in later life to the need to know where we come from and where we stand, where we are going, and who is going with us.

At any rate, only as I had completed my selection of Jefferson quotations (the sayings of a man impressively taller than most of his contemporaries and declared great in his own lifetime) did I notice that almost each one referred to the dimensions of the upright human body. You will remember his description of the Natural Bridge, "springing, as it were, up to heaven" so that the view from the top appeared to be painful and intolerable: "You involuntarily fall on your hands and feet [and] creep to the parapet." And then, there was the ludicrous argument started by French biologists over the bodily height of the American aborigines, the colonials, and slaves—an argument made more specific by references to the respective power that emanated from their heads, their hearts, and their genital organs. And then we heard Jefferson pursue, in his love letter, the pointed antagonism of head and heart, and the head's victory—at the price of a mysterious and damaging fall. The precariousness of human uprightness appeared in his warnings to his daughter concerning the "precipice of the gulph" that awaited those not "laborious." Add to this his suggestive reference to the divided functions of the right and the left hand, one of the many human peculiarities dependent on an upright posture facing forward, and it is as if, in a few quotations, we had marked a cross as symbolic of man's bodily existence: from head to foot, from left to right. *Ecce Homo.*

At the beginning, then, man is prone, looking up to the inclined and responsive face of the motherly person which smiles and frowns. And we will thereafter always look for somebody to look up to; and we will henceforth be confirmed as persons only if we are chosen by, uplifted, and, in fact, made to feel essential for that very person's own condition of elevation. This, a good leader provides for many adults, and their need as well as his seeming ability to stand alone are both fundamental for that much-discussed charisma. It renews hope and trust, the first virtues in life and the most persistently necessary: Without them we feel the dread of remaining both unguided and unrecognized in an empty universe.

As we begin to crawl, we learn to master a leeway permitting us to venture out into space just far enough to be able to crawl back. We learn to follow our willful heads to explore what is ahead, and to turn around to what, in back, has remained safely there.

A special threat of imbalance, however, and of standing all alone, comes with standing up and, thus, standing out. Let us look at some of the dimensions of this experience, and let me arouse your own pictorial and verbal associations as I line up some metaphorical descriptions which link bodily existence and inner life with spatial and social perspectives.

For the person who stands upright, the head, with its halo of light perception and consciousness is on top. The eyes are in front. Our vision, then, faces what is *ahead* and *in front*. What is *behind* is also *in back*. These are the beginnings of a unified space-time experience. And then there are combinations: ahead and above; ahead and below; behind and above; behind and below, all of which receive varied connotations during childhood. All languages abound in metaphors (systematically tied to each other) which indicate that these directions suggest both basic moods, such as elation and depression, and fundamental social relations. To play with a few: Ahead and above are those whom I hope someday to equal and who are yet sometimes hard to catch up with. I am delighted if they pick me up to their own height, and chagrined when they abruptly put me down, or eventually let me down. But because of the very fact that we are so largely oriented toward what is ahead and guided by what is above and points ahead, the dimensions of behind and below are of particular and often sinister importance. For no matter how we turn, in order to see what otherwise we could only hear, there is a behind which we can never face, and which yet can be seen and approached by others. Those who are behind me, then, fall into such contradictory categories as those who are backing me up, that is, encourage me to go ahead; or those who are after me, trying to get me from behind. (Children, of course, play with all these dangers, and while peek-a-boo may have helped them to get used to the disappearance of the face that promises to reappear, to be chased invites a pleasurable threat from behind, if only the child knows he will be reassured when caught.) Below and behind are those whom I simply may have outgrown. But then there are those things and people which I want to leave behind—forget, discard.

The association of the behind with elimination is especially strong and hostile. ("The British," said Jefferson, "are in our bowels and we must expel them.") The American language, of course, delights in calling those who are more than dispensable "shit." And we experience what may subversively waylay us ahead and below as vermin to be stepped on—an imagery used by our soldiers to explain their unsoldierly rage at My Lai.

What at first is the elated surprise of "I can stand!" someday—many crises later—becomes a proud "This is what I stand for," or maybe even a "Here I stand!" Basic, then, is a ground to stand on, and the capacity to be above lowness and baseness. To grow also means to outgrow others and, in fact, oneself; and in the process much that I once was and that others still are, will now be beneath me. But simple as they sound, all these perspectives underlie the complexity of space-time development: What I am in space, changes in time; what I was is now in me; and what I become is more than the sum of all that I have been.

In a similar vein one could, given enough time, start with other beginnings and go into other developmental directions: sensory and cognitive, muscular and locomotor, sexual and social. To mention only the most immediate, there is the differentiation of a right side and a left one, which is dictated by the forward orientation. The strong and dexterous right arm, too, is an evolutionary fact, embellished with such issues of man's social evolution as war and workmanship. It makes the right side righteous, and might, right. And it puts a high premium on the warrior and hunter and his sexual characteristics: What counts is to be out front, and to be well equipped up front. And then, there is sexual differentiation. Women and men share, of course, the upright posture and the forward orientation, as well as dexterity; but there can be little doubt that in the more primitive layers of our psyche the very ground plan of the human body has given an aggressive-defensive meaning to all development; and so during the childhood years when this upright perspective develops, sexual differences, too, take on lasting, irrational connotations. Such connotations attach to the beginnings of all the various ways in which upright creatures will engage each other: *Erotic encounters* prepare the patterns for intimacy, a sharing of the body's erogenous possibilities as well as of each other's innermost experience; *affiliative bonds* attest to the fact that one is sharing the same ground, employing the same techniques, moving toward common goals; while *antagonistic exclusions* represent a reversal of all these indices and enforce a defensive and offensive fortification of front, rear, and flank. How these basic patterns emerge and interact in a given cultural setting within the hierarchy of familial settings—that, we now know, has much to do with the basic expectations and fears with which the child and adolescent will first behold his wider, his political role.

Our main point is that each individual, being stamped with such early experiences in space and time, and at first sharing them with a small circle of familiar individuals, must seek an (eventually political) association with wider circles who share a basic world view: Their ideological space-time perspectives, we can now see, must alleviate for all what anxiety remains from the bodily ontogeny of each. But—we may now add—human anxiety always reflects the inner as well as the outer world, and so we must as yet briefly account for another evolutionary given, namely, the complementarity of inner and outer experience. For the growing, maturing, observing I is soon faced within, too, with a higher self that forever speaks for those who once were taller, wiser, or, at any rate, more powerful. If they, in bringing us up were always admonishing and punishing us, that is what our conscience, more or less benevolently, now does to us. We also have a lower self which we may enjoy with conspirational pleasure, until our higher self succeeds in making us see that we have, again, stooped too low. And we develop an ideal self that beckons us to take chances with a future in which we will become identical with those powerful parental figures. In its service, we will gladly forget some of our past selves and repress some especially awkward memories.

For all of these inner agencies psychoanalysis has, of course, technical terms. There is an ego ideal and a super ego; the latter (since we are paying attention to the American language today) does not mean an ego that makes me feel super, but quite on the contrary, a part of myself that lords it over me. But let me say a word about the ego itself. Again, in the American language, the person who has an ego has an overgrown self-esteem. In psychoanalysis, on the contrary, the ego is that balancing function in mental life which keeps things in perspective and in readiness for action. With the help of a sound nervous system, it mediates between outer events and inner responses, between past and future, and between the higher and the lower selves. Above all, the ego works at all times on the maintenance of a sense that we (and that means, each of us) are central in the flux of our experience ,and not tossed around on some periphery; that we are original in our plans of action instead of being pushed around; and, finally, that we are active and, in fact, are activating (as well as being activated by) others instead of being made passive or being inactivated by exigencies. All this together makes the difference between feeling (and acting) whole—or fragmented. Obviously, to convince itself of such a position, each ego must maintain a certain sense of omnipotence as well as omniscience which, if not kept within the bounds of the shared omnipotencies and omnisciences of a joint world view will, in the long run, make us criminal or insane. No ego is an island to itself; and, indeed, as we saw, the language we learn as we stand up and grow up, transmits to each the common experience of all: I, you, we—in the same world of facts, of experience, and of interaction.

But let us face it, this our pride, our organ of adaptation and of adjustment, is also the seat of man's corruptibility; and so, at the end, one must grant that the popular use of the term *ego* which ascribes to it a certain egotism and grandiosity, has its point. As adulthood arrives we have learned to identify with those whom we find above us in the political and metaphysical order; to accept laws which help us subdue what to ourselves has become beneath ourselves; and to project on others what in ourselves now appears as small and weak, bad and sick, or driven by desires we had to repudiate. Thus each ego, and often the very one we would, indeed, call healthy or strong, persistently explores the borderlines of what it can get away with—with itself and with others. In the form of the defense mechanisms classically described by Anna Freud, it learns to make deals with itself which work up to a point; and, of course, the respective egos of persons living closely together learn to make deals with, and against, each other. We must learn to understand the worst of this, and yet remain mindful that collusion can mean anything from artfully playing up to each other to corrupting each other, even as making deals can mean giving one another an even chance or stacking the cards against each other. To engage in interplay, to give and gain leeway, to increase the sum

total of mutual good will and of insight—these are the ego's
great gifts from the gods.

* * *

We are now at the midpoint of the second lecture, and it
is time to decide what in all this we wish to call political.
For clinical literature and literature gone clinical for purposes of persuasion has recently begun to use the word
political for all interpersonal dealings, as if a person could
play politics with his inner selves, and a number of persons (in a family, for example) with each other. This can
be strikingly enlightening where it demonstrates that what
has been studied as the inner economy of single persons is
really (or also) an ecology of interrelations. But it seems
important to reserve the word *political* (without quotation
marks) for man's polis, for his capacity to build and imagine communities (from the concrete town to the city of
God) which not only take care of the necessities of daily
life but also can have an exquisite style maintaining, at its
best, a creative interplay with man's inner life. Thus man's
higher self receives meaning from, as it gives meaning to,
the elite of his polity, even as his ideal and his lower selves
are meaningfully reflected in the public drama of his society's heroes and outlaws. His ego, in turn, is supported
by the fraternity of cocitizenship in which his identity
can feel at home. No disparaging or pamphleteering use
of the word *political* should detract from these fundamental needs and capacities; although it must be clear that each
of them is peculiarly corruptible.

A science of politics, informed by psychology, would,
then, provide explanations for the dangerous affinity to
each other of the most corrupt and the most virtuous in
man. And I daresay, that close to the ground as the themes

just related are, you may, here and there, have perceived their applicability to events in this city of Washington and in high places. For rarely have we been so aware of the pervasive power of atavistic strivings, and of how the man out front, the erstwhile warrior and hunter, has perpetuated himself not only in war but also in business as well as in politics, while his stance of domination becomes somewhat more subtle in the professions and, of course, in the arts and sciences.

But let me conclude my remarks on ontogeny by returning to the problem of identity. It is, of course, in adolescence that those configurations of engagement develop by which childhood experience is translated into new encounters and into action. Youth joins the symbolic with the passionate by linking arms and embracing, by marching together, by working and praying side by side, by joining in rhythmic movement, and by opposing each other in games. Thus are clarified the patterns I spoke of: erotic intimacy, affiliative loyalty, and also the passion of excluding others, that is, of knowing against what and whom one will stand and fall together. But all this can only emerge convincingly within some ideological vision—and ideological, to me, is a developmental necessity not monopolized by political parties. At any rate, it may become clear to us now, how the most unlettered individual, on the mere basis of how he grew up to be what he now becomes, has a deep investment in such principles as, for example, that all citizens stand free, and all stand equally high, while all stand together against those who think they are more equal than others and who manipulate facts, fictionalize reality, and corrupt interaction.

Here Jefferson's assumption and that of his friends that

there is in man in principle a moral core that, if given leeway to manifest itself in mutual activation with others
will tend to make ethical and rational choices, represents a
basic developmental truth. One may be more impressed
with the chaotic and regressive or committed and forward
looking, the withdrawn and dreaming, or passionate and
competent stance of adolescence. But it is at this stage and
in the confluence of the internalized reality with the political world, that childhood ideals attach themselves to
patterns of work and to ideological verities embodied in
forms of collaboration and leadership. Thus it will be decided whether or not the individual will have a chance to
transform what is left of his infantile guilt and rage into
communal activity of lasting value to him and others.

It is easy enough and, up to a point, necessary for leaders
to offer to youth, as well as to the perennial adolescent in
adults, some overdefined enemies *against whom* to maintain a sense of identity. Nowhere does the quality of leadership become more apparent than in the interplay of the
inner deals the leader makes with himself and the inner
deals he thinks he can count on in those he leads. For this
will decide what kind of political deals he thinks he can
offer to his constituents. And, as we suggested, the most
sensitive question in this joint arena of inner worlds is the
double role of conscience as a benevolent and experienced
guide and as a punitive, condemning inner tyrant. What,
in the name of all that is holy, we are ready to repress in
ourselves and whom, in the name of what we have killed in
ourselves, we are ready to annihilate in the world at large—
that is the most fateful human question.

All this, of course, is essentially related to that process of
creating mythological entities which I spoke of as pseudo-

species—that is, tribes and nations, creeds and classes, each of which makes like being the human race with a glorious and ceremonially hallowed vision of itself. This has offered youth, in its ideological hunger, causes to live and to die for, and has attracted its heroism and self-sacrifice in periodical wars with other pseudospecies, foreign or domestic. In fact, when I first discussed the notion of pseudospeciation, Konrad Lorenz suggested that it was indispensable to man's periodical urge to annihilate some of his own species, a habit which he claimed was foreign to honest animals in authentic evolution. Today, all war threatens to be war on the species itself; and it is, therefore, deeply meaningful that, as never before, in wide circles of the Western world, the ritualization of warfare, as centered in the identity of honor, is losing its primary appeal, while mobilizations for peace can attract the supranational loyalties of many. But, then, in recent history, the most colossal pseudospecies of them all, the technologically advanced modern nations have shown themselves willing to fight world wars and indulge in mass annihilations—no doubt, in some fear of losing traditional corporate identities. If, at this time, I suggest that we study in great detail the relationship of those simplest inner deals which we make with ourselves, and the political deals which we acquiesce in or feel inspired by, I hope that you will give me the benefit of the doubt that I am as aware as is the next man, of the overweening power of territorial facts and economic forces, and of all kinds of accidents in political transformations— although in two lectures I cannot apply the themes suggested to concrete historical events.

Permit me, instead, to conclude this discussion of bodily symbolism by relating most briefly the earliest memory I have of the mood of this country, in the days of my immigration, the early thirties. It was the time of the New Deal. Here was a great and wealthy country having undergone a traumatic economic depression which, as I can now see, must have seemed to paralyze that very self-made identity and put into question its eternal renewal. At that lowest period, a leader appeared who himself could not stand on his own feet because, alas, he was paralyzed from the waist down. But on the arm of a son or an aide, he appeared always erect; and as his mood seemed to belie the catastrophe that had befallen him, and as his voice ringingly rose above any emotional depression, he was able to lift the spirit of the masses, and they marched—behind the man in the wheelchair. Happy days were here again.

This sounds like a fable, and it is not meant to be much more than that, for it obviously neglects all economic and political factualities. But a fable does not lie, and this one certainly did have reality in those times, even as later it helped to activate the nation against the greatest danger to mankind's painfully slow progress toward unity: fascism. That Roosevelt and the mythological scientific figure of his time, that Roosevelt and Einstein united in the initiation of the age of nuclear destruction—that is another chapter in our slow and zigzagging road toward the realization of specieshood for which the creation of an American identity may well be one significant model.

Crisis of the Identity Crisis

THE NEW IDENTITY, born on this continent, emerged not only from liberties secured by revolution, but also from the courage of a new, a truly original consciousness. If you now expect—either from a mood of hope or from one of challenge—that I will outline in a few easy last pages the shape and substance of a new new identity to come, I hope you will remember that in this moment of our national history we do not have any of the clear territorial and institutional givens which—as it seems in retrospect— formed such a convincing background for the old new identity of our founding fathers. On the contrary, the imperative need of a disengagement from such adventures as the war in Southeast Asia and our tortuous and tortured response to it only indicates how difficult it is to accommodate ourselves to the overweening fact that the geopolitical foundations of the American identity have changed beyond recognition. As the imagery of the new continent is fading, so is that of the frontier, of the halls of Montezuma and the shores of Tripoli, and of Iwo Jima. To leave Vietnam behind, means not only to come to our senses in regard to the national identity we inherited with our constitutional liberties, but also to gain further insight into our motivational human bondage. Nothing less is at stake now than the *inner liberation* necessary to plan the global politics of a technology shared by one species. Such policies begin with the prevention of global destruction: will they find fulfillment in a universal world view which takes each child along on spaceship earth? In this context I can do no more than to trace (in terms of the concepts at my disposal) some of the *inner hindrances* to mankind's attempts to liberate itself—so that our talk of liberty may not ever again sound like a record with the needle stuck in one groove, sickeningly repeating a fragment of a melody just when we expect its consummation.

When I spoke of an old new identity, I implied something like this; for an identity based on newness must get in its own way when it begins to repeat itself. But, then, this newness, from the beginning, had its counterpoint in a need for sedentary sameness—with a vengeance. And, indeed, a sense of continuous selfhood always demands a balance between the wish to hold on to what one has proven to be and the hope to be renewed—a dimension of identity which at all times makes urgent a division between conservative, if not reactionary, and liberal, if not radical, versions of a given world view.

But what if, as seems to have happened in America, a whole new civilization is conscious of creating itself? And what if such preoccupation leads to a kind of self-consciousness first apparent in its literature, and eventually also in its psychology, surely beginning with William James? If such awareness eventually includes a special acceptance of problems of identity—which, in themselves, so I would insist, are universal and necessary—does not such special awareness interfere with the innocence of the process itself? Or could it be that our special curiosity concerning unconscious motivation is itself a further development of an evolutionary need for an ever-more conscious core of self-sameness in the acceleration of technological and scientific change?

Since our insight into problems of identity, like so many other fundamental insights, has originated in clinical thought, let me say here a word about Freud. We have learned to take it for granted that a neuropsychiatrist has become one of the great enlightening influences in the Western world. Each age, of course, has its own idea of what liberates inner man, and I have, in these lectures, pointed to an over-all trend in the conceptualization of inner unfreedom. I quoted in detail a Gospel passage emphasizing the sufferer's faith as the decisive factor in her cure. Turning to Jefferson's time, I reported how Rush, trained in Europe, gained remarkable insights into mental dynamics. He anticipated Freud when, for example, he claimed that depression "may be induced by causes that are forgotten; or by the presence of objects which revive the sensation of distress with which at one time it was associated, but without reviving the cause of it in the memory." These brief illustrations, so distant from each other in time and context, may yet indicate a trend which more and more places the cause of mental disturbance in the victim's inner life and its cure in an inner resolve—according to Rush's advice, to keep clean and busy. Freud's moral as well as clinical sense made him, too, discard the laying on of hands which was still done in hypnosis, and remove himself from any other role of authority except the voice that encourages insight into the cause of the distress and helps such insight along by interpretation. But the idea of a disturbing quantity remained: Some evil substance which in the Gospels was driven into swine, in Rush's time was still let out with bad blood and today is shocked out electrically. In Freud's time, too, there was the idea of a cathartic experience, the abreaction of imprisoned emotion. But here it was to serve the facilitation of insight, that is the utilization of the patient's own ego strength for his own transformation. Thus, in helping another set of outcasts (the hysterics that Jefferson had held up warningly to his daughter) to respect themselves and to understand their own history, he created methods and concepts applicable not only to all kinds of deviants, but to the history of so-called normal man himself. By this means he extended man's responsibility for his own unconscious and especially for the development of his children by lifting the repression that had beclouded and falsified early development. And so he made possible a certain foresight in regard to the generational processes in which Jefferson was so passionately interested. He did so by replacing some previously erratic hindsight with systematic insight.

But Freud was also the first thinker to predict that such new findings as his could by the very nature of things never be accepted without an inner resistance which, in fact, he considered part of the normal workings of the mind. So we are, or we should be, prepared for the fact that such resistances join other defensive reactions against insights which seem to rob us of our self-made certainty. Freud, in this respect, compared his own ideas with those of Copernicus and Darwin as "disturbers of mankind's sleep"; I think that we must add to this illustrious list Marx, and Freud's contemporary, Einstein.

In fact, I would nominate the idea of relativity in the physical world and the concept of the unconscious in man's inner world (and I include in this Marx's discovery of a class unconscious) as two such disturbing extensions of human consciousness in our time. And I would postulate that any new identity must develop the *courage of its relativities* and the *freedom of its unconscious resources;* which includes facing the anxiety aroused by both. Man always reprojects on himself what he has managed to conceptualize in the universe; history teaches what theories of the universe come to mean to everyday man. And relativity has come to suggest relativism—an idea, of course, foreign to Einstein. But then, you may remember, or I do, that even outstanding German scientists in Einstein's time considered his work *abscheulich*—repugnant. It gave them a moral shudder. Gerald Holton rightly corrects them and us: "Relativity Theory," he says, "of course, does not find that truth depends on the point of view of the observer but, on the contrary, reformulated the laws of physics so that they hold good for every observer, no matter *how he moves or where he stands.* Its central meaning is that the most valued truths in science are wholly independent of the point of view." I have italicized the words which should remind us of the psychological importance of a *standpoint* in order to clarify the paradoxical relationship between major scientific upheavals and the human ego's aforementioned criteria: centrality, originality, choice, initiative—and identity. Centrality seems endangered if the earth is not in the center of the universe; originality, if we are descended from a lower species; choice and initiative, if what we think we are doing is decisively influenced by unconscious motivation. Thus new facts, demonstrated by men who can play with facts with utmost sincerity, and who, in their competence and certainty have the courage to stand alone and can thus risk both sanity and acceptance, often seem to shatter what we continue to think must be real. The paradox is that these facts and theories increase human power over nature (and human nature) enormously, but create a lag between what we know and what we can "realize"—a dangerous situation, indeed.

In response to this new consciousness, there are many reactions. Some are joyful and resourceful, creating a new leeway in inventiveness and thoughtfulness; but I think it is my task to point, rather, to the age-old extremes of too narrow and too wide identities. There is, then, the attempt to preserve the old new identity that contends all the more grimly that one can and must be consciously self-made, fabricated, a do-it-yourself personality in the American tradition, a tradition which permits a kind of old-fashioned stance actually relying on the reactionary possession of privileged interests and organized powers. This old new identity is marked by a disdainful punitiveness toward those who, instead, experiment with different identities, and this at their own pace.

Among the young—or now not so young anymore—there are those who mistrust the whole identity concept as another trick of the older generation, designed to impose traditional restraints on what one might become if one refused to make anything of oneself and merely continued to improvise, to drift. These young people seem to to be permissive toward themselves and disdainful primarily toward those who believe so strenuously that they know who they are. But this does not mean that they are not seeking what they are denying. For even where new forms of consciousness and new social patterns arise in bewildering alternation, the fundamental need for a familiar identity, as we saw, changes ever so slowly. And so, the search for a revolutionary identity often leads to stances belonging to other eras and bygone proletariats.

Identity is safest, of course, where it is grounded in activities. When we meet a new person, we usually want to know what he does, and then, how he does what he does. For a need for competence, too, is well anchored in development, and most importantly, the stage of identity grows out of the school age, that is, the stage when work competence and gamesmanship emerge out of the matured ability to play meaningfully, and, in play and work, to entertain ideal images of initiative. But such ideals of future competence always remain beset with some infantile guilt over the usurpation of roles previously occupied by parental figures; and the question is always whether such a subjective usurpation will find sanction in a competence of performance verified by the objective nature of things. For this reason, a new identity will be very much attached to an intimate mastery of a set of skills dictated by the state of science and technology as well as the arts, and no attempt to humanize life should belittle or bedevil this mastery itself. Competence without conviction, to be sure, is not more than a form of fact-slavery; but conviction without competence is less than liberation.

It is interesting in this connection how some of the most sincere rebels among our young felt the need for activities on the land or in the crafts in order to touch base with what grows and what responds with unfailing honesty. Yet, the notion that everything is relative has undoubtedly contributed to the character of contemporary identity formation in many subtle as well as blatant ways. In my first lecture, I discussed the fact that Jefferson was a man naturally referred to as a Protean man, that is, one who could wear (to use his own phrase) a number of seemingly contradictory characters in one lifetime: farmer and architect, rebel and aristocrat, statesman and philosopher, American and classicist—not to speak of seemingly contradictory personal traits including a certain mixture of what impresses as feminine and masculine. But in all this he was always himself. And he was a member and a leader of a time which invited changeability and multiplicity even as it also invited a steadfastness of character—without quotation marks. In saying a few words about the general emergence in our day of a Protean man encouraged by the spread of American manners it may be well to remember Proteus' predicament. He knew the past, the present, and the future of all things, and it was in order to avoid having to tell that truth that he assumed the pseudo identities of animals and elements of nature. Only when caught napping and held down before he could escape into different beings was he forced to be himself and tell what he knew. So there was a real and lasting Proteus in the original Protean personality, a tragic core-identity in the multiplicity of elusive roles.

But what if role-playing becomes an aim in itself, is rewarded with success and status, and seduces the person to repress what core-identity is potential in him? Even an actor is convincing in many roles only if and when there is in him an actor's core-identity—and craftsmanship. Comparably, there may well be some character types who thrive on Protean possibilities, even as there is, by definition, a developmental period (namely, youth) when the experimentation with a range of roles and alternating states of mind, can be a way of personal growth. What is described as a Protean personality today may, in fact, be an attempt on the part of adolescent personalities—and America has always cultivated them—to adjust to overwhelming change by a stance of deliberate changeability, of maintaining the initiative by playing at change so as to stay ahead of the game. We will be our own or one another's fathers and mothers, confirm each other's identities, form our own traditions; and what is more, we can do all this over and over again. Those who are gifted in this game, and, therefore, truly playful in it, may with luck make it an essential part of their identity formation and find a new sense of centrality and originality in the flux of our time. But how, we must ask, will these Proteans face their own progeny? Could not their wish forever to reproduce versions of themselves permit them to repress the adult wish to produce (or to care for) new beings—a denial easily rationalized by reference to the necessity to limit the world's population?

Whereas for Proteus, then, multiple identity was a matter of tragic fate, and whereas for us—who attempt to think in relativities as well as in unconscious meanings—it should become a matter of more conscious and better-informed choice, it often turns today into a matter of obsession. For example, instead of a freer and more individual

choice, all forms of sexuality previously marked as repressed, or as perverse, are now being enacted as if their
mere alternation amounted to sexual freedom. No wonder
that the playing out of these and other interchangeable roles
can often give a fleeting sense of identity only when rein-
forced by drugs which help to dull diffuse guilt.

I have said enough today about the nature of human
conscience to indicate that where roles, in the name of
multiple identity or of none, are played out licentiously,
the old-fashioned conscience is not liberated, but re-
repressed. And the consequence is not greater freedom in
informed permissiveness but an inability to personify and to
convey to others any ethics except that of making a variety
of role adjustments instead of a single one. And adjustment
is not enough. The ego demands adaptation both in the
sense of adaptedness and in that of adapting the human
environment to human needs; wherefore, the relationship
of work (which does not necessarily mean class) patterns
and identity remains decisive, and with it the mutual adaptation of technological mastery and the human life cycle.

But to return to the other extreme, the new punitiveness
which is based on the grim old identity and promoted with
a barely dissembled combination of vindictiveness and bad
conscience—for you can always be sure that the loudest
moralists have made deals with their own consciences—
such punitiveness seems to be more satisfying to the vindi-
cator and self-vindicator than helpful in the solution of law-
lessness. We should know that where large numbers of
young persons can find a moment of heightened identity
only in a flaunting of the negative identity, whether in
shiftlessness or in crime, in lone criminality or in the
abortive communality of gangs, that their capacity to

make informed choices has been atrophied by social neglect; and there are always—besides the availability of cheap weapons—plenty of violent and ruthless pseudo ideals displayed in the media and by the establishment itself to make vindictive stances fashionable. Instead of incarcerating so many young people in a manner sure to stultify their moral initiative altogether, we should be examining the influence on youth of official demonstrations of reckless superior power weakly rationalized by superior necessity, and yet indicative mainly of the superior need for self-vindication. It is clear that no new identity can emerge without a moral authority which, by an informed justice, restores to the person who has impulsively transgressed a maximum of informed choice. And we believe with Jefferson that where there is a choice and where there is relevant and shared information, most young persons will be inclined to choose productive companionship over lonely criminality.

In the end, this too poses a political question arising from the deals the various caretakers of justice make with themselves and their copractitioners, and the deals society makes with itself by acquiescing in and colluding with the complexity of legalities which serve as convenient disguises for a self-vindication in no way indicative of moral authority.

I seem to refer here primarily to young deviants, those who belong to the supposedly living generation. If I now seem to link together young deviants of very different motivational and legal status, it is not in order to point up similarities in them, but in our attitudes toward them as scapegoats. After the cease-fire in Southeast Asia a marked regrouping of the national imagery of heroes and villains was most noticeable: The returned prisoners of war, almost all career military men, were feted; the masses of returning draftees were all but ignored; and those who had refused to be drafted, or had deserted, were marked as villains permanently beyond amnesty. Many of these young dissenters, being young, and being forced to serve national policies openly disavowed by many citizens and held to be a national embarrassment by almost all, had no choice but to personify the growing resistance; and now we debate whether to forgive them or to forget their deed. All this, someday, will be studied as part of the shifts in propagandistic and emotional responses to the various phases of the war. My emphasis, right here, is on the readiness to exclude from national life young people who, one way or another, bear the brunt of our conflicts. Could it be that we keep some incarcerated behind prison walls and others excarcerated beyond our borders, in order to avoid facing either those sinister impulses or those high ideals which led them to deviate? I have indicated that the putting behind bars of many who were denied any living alternative to crime, and the external banishment of many who had no alternative but to refuse national service—is reminiscent of the way in which we, the adjusted, repress in ourselves our worst potentials and our best, in order not to endanger our adjustment. But as we limit our own personality by refusing to face the worst and the best in us, so we vastly impoverish our nation by excluding from the lifestream of the community the youthful energies of so many—and this in the name of honor, or law, or order.

I will not reiterate the relation of inner repression to outer suppresion. But I think that recent developments in our national life such as the sudden shift of attention from military atrocity in foreign lands to political scandal at home, and then the dramatic public display of individuals responsible for or caught in such scandal, should leave no doubt about the psychological relationships I have only been able to sketch here: namely, that between the *repression* of inner conflict in those who overadjust to power, the *suppression* of adversary opinions, and the ready *oppression* of foreign people. May we learn to keep this interrelatedness in full view, and not be distracted by what satisfies vindictiveness or self-vindication most sensationally at a given "point in time."

In the meantime, we may ponder that at this point in history this country must come to grips with its own awareness of historical guilt, over having transgressed against humanity and nature. Yet, it may find it difficult, for reasons of its own history, even to contemplate such exigence. To acknowledge universal sin, most democratically, is a different matter: That all too many find all too easy to do—once a week. But to recognize the potential of hubris in an expansive initiative which by its very material success seemed to be its own best justification (even as the invasion of foreign countries was for their own good) will truly call for a new identity. Contrition, as we have seen, is not an American virtue, and, indeed, mere contrition could admit everything, and change nothing. To find culprits is more our style; but culprits, in taking their punishment, take our part of the guilt with them. Liberation can come only from insights into the relevance of past guilt and into the place of ethical choice in the reformation of identity.

Liberation and Insight

I HAVE NOW pointed to a number of atavistic trends in man, first linking the concept of pseudospeciation with Jefferson's passionate and diffident attemtps to liberate himself from prejudices then apparently vindicated by the knowledge available to him and yet experienced as a human tragedy. At that time he seems to have needed for his new consciousness the certainty that white is beautiful, and that the nobility of emotion he saw in the white face guaranteed both moral power and restraint in the usurpation of power. It took, alas, a civil war and almost two centuries to secure for black citizens not only some of the most elementary liberties but also a measure of inner liberation that enabled them to convince themselves and others that black is beautiful—and competent. Yet their liberties as well as their liberation are progressing so slowly that at times only jetlike rebellion seemed to accelerate things noticeably.

It makes sense, I think, to differentiate between liberty and liberation and (as I meant to indicate in the title of these lectures) between the revolutionary actions which secure the first, and the inner emancipation that frees the second. A worldwide new identity, one suspects, eventually will have to liberate itself (an idea not foreign to Marx) from the variety of revolutionary patterns by which liberties were first secured, and from their moralistic fervor, puritan or radical.

Let me, in conclusion, apply some of the concepts presented here to the liberation movements of today, and this in the sequence of their having taken the center of national attention. The Black, the young, and the female have one experience in common: They have been the others, where the adult white male has been "it." And there is an intrinsic, an in-built psychological unfreedom in all groups characterized by stigmata which mark an irreversible difference from a dominant type, an unfreedom not resolved by the mere promise of political and economic equality—although, of course, impossible without it. For built into the demand for liberty is the (more or less) subdued rage of centuries over having been peripheral to the central spot in a new world image. It is as simple and as fateful as this: A black, if ever so equal, could not choose to turn into a white; an adolescent, if ever so sure of a future adulthood, could not choose to have it now and his way; and a woman, even when a complete equal, could not choose to have been born a man. But they who cannot choose to be different, cannot decide freely to remain what they are. In this predicament it does not help to point out that the white male adult could not choose to be otherwise either; and that, worse, he learned in childhood that he must not even play or dream that eventually he might want to be anything but a white male adult. And it is true that the dominant male type in all societies (and here I include all modern states) is offered special chances and privileges in order to make him define his own identity in the narrow and uniform terms demanded by the system.

In the recent revolts and protests in the West, youth-conscious youth, to rid itself of the onus of being a pseudo-species defined by its birth date decided to declare a pseudo-speciation across nations, classes, and religions. The older generation was now treated as a kind of outcast species and only being young promised a new identity and a new personhood. To testify as a writer: I had to become aware of the fact that the identity crisis was a welcome concept not (or not only) because it made developmental sense as a transitional stage—which I will not deny—but because it helped to glorify the drama of youth, with all its dangers, as a semipermanent state quite desirable on its own terms.

To write about womanhood is a different matter; and I would like to concentrate briefly on women's liberation, just because the reference in my title to the new identity rather than the new man, could make us forget too easily that, finer linguistic points notwithstanding, the new man did, and does, in the minds of men and women, mean the self-made male. In fact, once this is acknowledged, one suspects that self-made implies a male denial of having been born and raised by women: Who needs to be raised, if he can pull himself up by his bootstraps?—and this in a world created by a man God, and perfected by founding fathers.

Having been glorified in a most ambivalent manner by both yankees and cavaliers it is not too astonishing, then,

that women in search of a new consciousness mistrust
writers like myself, who must base conclusions concerning
women's very special superiorities on the claim that there
are (some) sexual differences.

Here, too, a new consciousness, for a while, needed new
pseudospeciation: the now so obvious fact that women had,
indeed, been treated as the other sex was countered by de-
bates in which, at last, women could openly speak of men
as the other human kind. (Incidentally, when bad came to
very worse, all liberation movements seem to agree on one
animal species that likes to wallow in mud as the appropriate counterspecies to liken the adult white male to.) Gone
was the understanding, which men need so desperately,
that iron tradition as well as the fear of symbolic castra-
tion has driven them into a speciation full of anxious ambition and boring drudgery as well as welcome work; full
of the danger of failure as well as of the chance of getting
to the top; and, above all, linked to the commitment to
serve as the drafted executioners as well as the maimed vic-
tims of warfare.

If the first step of liberation is the liberty not to be what
others say one must be, so that one may be free to find a
self-chosen form of being what one is, then, the promises
of femaleness diminish before Freud's famous and now
notorious dictum that anotomy is destiny. And, indeed,
this dictum has an interesting psychohistorical history, for
with it, Freud meant to contradict Napoleon the con-
queror's motto that history is destiny. While I (and others)
would not deny either of these destinies, our identity consciousness would make us add that personality, too, is decisive and that destiny, for both men and women, depends
on what you can make of the fact that you have a specific
kind of body in a particular historical setting; and making

something of that fact certainly includes the right to rebel against what others make of it. Yet any emphasis on a particular kind of body is, as some writers have made very clear, resented as truly un-American, because the American identity has played into a very deep human need by glorifying the unlimited choice of self-made roles and personalities.

When I, among the stages of life, postulated the development of initiative at the transition from the play age to the school age—an initiative which has to free itself from infantile guilt—some critics questioned the term *initiative* as emphasizing too American a value. And while I do believe that all human beings develop some forms of initiative sanctioned by their culture and limited by some defined guilt, it is also obvious that the American identity put a special premium on this quality of action which well fits the general need for newness. Such premium, however, is denied to those who are limited in their initiative; in fact, there is every indication that classes of individuals deprived of initiative can feel guilty—as if something in themselves had caused their deprivation. The natural way to dispose of such self-accusation is to take the initiative in accusing others with a moralistic outrage which, however, may soon exhaust itself and hinder rather than help competent action.

A certain rage of protest is a necessary fuel for setting liberation, or at any rate, vindication, in motion. But the process, once under way, needs a new consciousness not served by a re-repression of the obvious. It desperately needs shared insights into the inner collusion of those discriminated against with their habitual discriminators. I have pointed to one of the well-known inner deals on the side of those discriminated against: It is, as would follow from the joint existence in a shared world image, not only an acceptance of the dominant ideal, but also an unconscious agreement with the judgment of inferiority, and this for the sake of what in my field is called secondary gain.

The world image that put the self-made man in the center of the universe assigned to the woman certain complementary roles so powerful in the private and educative sphere, that they served as compensation for both sexes: It allowed the men to feel dominated, and, in fact, to invite private domination, and it allowed women to renounce other spheres of power and to neglect potential competencies. In the agricultural beginning in small town settings, of course, there had at first been a distribution of functions that gave to divided roles at least one equality: an assignment to both sexes of equally unremitting and equally essential work. Such role divisions were later transferred to entirely different economic settings, and led to the acceptance of unequal opportunity and unequal compensation. But the more self-madeness shifted in its emphasis from what you were (that is, made of yourself by hard work) to what you had (that is, acquired and conspicuously possessed) to what you could consume (that is, buy and use up) the more the woman's role at least in some dominant classes became symbolic for ostentatious display in such types as lady of the house, Mom, or ravishing playmate. The point is that where such roles confined women to circumscribed settings and activities, they also gave them a power denied to many men in the spheres wide open to them. Any liberating shift in world image, then, demands the joint study of such reciprocal accommodations.

And liberation, too, is always reciprocal. In fact, the

chance for true liberation occurs when both sides need it. Technological, commercial, and professional overexpansion threaten to make of men, too, caricatures of their one-sided masculinity as surely as the roles of housekeeper, guardian of manners, or mannequin, have exploited feminine propensities. In rebuilding the economic and political structure in order to accommodate both the equality of work opportunity and the shared functions of parenthood, it is necessary for men also to recognize the disguises under which they continue to play the role of self-made men where, in fact, they, too, are being had by their roles. Men may now recognize the obsession with the game of unlimited expansion where it has long led to an overextension of goals. They may see through the attempts to hide a habitual corruption of means under a guise of clever foresight. For the obvious cost of all this have been a mechanization of motives and an impoverishment of personality robbing lifetimes of that pursuit of happiness which, at the beginning, was the main idea.

Conclusion: A Century of the Adult?

A FINAL QUESTION, or rather two. When I was younger, there was much talk about the century of the child. Has it ended? We hope it has quietly joined the era. Since then we have gone through something like a century of youth. But when, pray, is the century of the adult to begin? Here, it seems to me, some questions have remained open. And yet, our knowledge of children as well as of young people will remain rather fragmentary (to them as well as to us) if we do not know what we would like them to become, or even what we would like to be—or to have been. Without this we feel vaguely guilty, whether we are permissive or punitive. Feeling guilty, we will overdo both. And let us face it, no statistical proof and no checklist as to what is good or bad for children or for youth will tell us how to be ourselves which, to them, seems to count most.

I happen to belong to a study group which attempts to find out what an adult is, which means, first, what an adult was supposed to be in different eras of history and in different areas of the world, and then, what an adult is and genuinely wants to be, today. You may or may not be surprised to hear how embarrassed and even a bit annoyed some of the most erudite and pragmatic individuals in many walks of life can be when asked to help us with such questions. "I have never thought about this, and I do not intend to start now," was one answer from a mature observer of politics. Some of our correspondents, of course, are embarrassed by our question because they do think that they are pretty adult, but would not wish to brag. Others who are not quite so sure may fear to be found out —as if we were so sure! But I think we are all up against the question as to what adults can mean to each other and to themselves in the working world to come, and especially so considering the fact that the children to be born from here on will have every right to ask why they were chosen to be born by free agreement if, indeed, the responsible adults do not know or care what ideals they can personify for them, or what choices they can give them.

Although the word *adult* comes from *adultus* and *adolescent* from *adolescentulus*, both masculine, the adulthood of the future must obviously be defined as joint, shared, and interdependent.

The choice to procreate or not, however, remains a free choice only if we cease to deny the psychobiological fact that matured sexuality is part of generativity. Mankind can play with any and all drives and use them for the glory of being alive, of being together, and of being creative; and yet, in the long run, it will have to account for them. To know that adulthood is generative, does not necessarily mean that one must produce children. But it means to know what one does if one does not. And it means that one participates otherwise in the establishment, the guidance, and the enrichment of the living generation and the world it inherits. The right (or the obligation) to have fewer children (or none) can only be a liberated one if it means a greater personal and communal responsibility for all those born, and the application of parental concerns to the preservation of what enhances the whole cycle of life.

Which reminds me, once more, of Jefferson's idea of the ideal size of a township. He may not have been so far off in regard to the optimal communal units to be built into a future megalopolis (except that bicycle paths rather than footwalks may there be the healthy measure of optimal surroundings). The main point is that at each stage of life there must be a network of direct personal and communal communication safely set within the wider networks of automobility and mass media. A spontaneous readiness for such community forming is noticeable all over the country and is reaching onto the architects' drawing boards. Such a need is felt, I believe, for good political as well as psychological reasons: American democracy, if it is to survive within the superorganizations of government and commerce, of industry and labor, is predicated on personal contacts within groups of optimal size—optimal meaning the power to persuade each other in matters that influence the lives of each. Nowhere is the power of women as workers more mandatory than in the communal culture of the future, for women, in all of mankind's existence, have learned to respond to the measure of the developing child, to the measure of the child in the adult, and to the measure of manageable communalities within wider communities. Men, of course, can learn much of this, if they only want to and this not only because they, too, had mothers and each has a mother in him, but simply because concern flourishes where permitted to do so.

But now I have only one minute left to indicate what an adult is. Identity, you may be glad to hear, is not everything, either for a person or a nation—once you have it, of course. I have attempted to indicate certain trends in how America came to have one. Yet a persistent concern over identity leads either to bragging or to complaining —bragging that one knows exactly who one is, as many national types (and caricatures) do so blatantly, or complaining that one does not. From the point of view of development, I would say: In youth you find out what you *care to do* and who you *care to be*—even in changing roles. In young adulthood you learn whom you *care to be with*— at work and in private life, not only exchanging intimacies, but sharing intimacy. In adulthood, however, you learn to know what and whom you can *take care of*. I have said all this in basic American before; but I must add that as a principle it corresponds to what in Hinduism is called the maintenance of the world, that middle period of the life cycle when existence permits you and demands you to consider death as peripheral and to balance its certainty with the only happiness that is lasting: to increase, by whatever is yours to give, the good will and the higher order in your sector of the world. That, to me, can be the only adult meaning of that strange word *happiness* as a political principle. What Jefferson said about the limit of the debts that should be inherited by the living generation—as well as the other quotations we underscored—could well include the hope that adults will learn to help each other not to burden the next generation with the immaturities which they themselves inherited from previous generations. And Jefferson, one could summarize, could not have been as great (and yet tragically aware) a figure, were it not for the inner circumstance that the oppressive conscience which he shared with past generations was in important respects balanced by ideal images personified in his youth by genuinely adult and competent figures. This, I believe, is the most poignant lesson for today of any restudy of such a man.

There is a new greeting around these days which, used casually, seems to suggest not much more than that we should be careful, or take care of ourselves. I would hope that it could come to mean more and I therefore want to conclude these lectures with it: TAKE CARE.

The Jefferson Lecture on the Humanities

IN 1972 the National Endowment for the Humanities established the Jefferson Lecture in the Humanities, a distinguished lecture series designed to help bridge the gap between scholarship and public affairs. For its annual lecture the Endowment commissions thinkers of international reputation to bring their learning and experience to bear on contemporary concerns. The lecturer addresses himself to aspects of contemporary culture, concerning himself with human values, goals, needs, and experiences, the central concerns of the humanities.

The lecture was named for Thomas Jefferson, President of the American Philosophical Society as well as third President of the United States. As much as any American who ever lived, he epitomized the scholar in touch with his own time, the man of learning to whom the present was the past unfinished. With Jefferson as symbol, the Endowment wishes to give leadership in affirming the relationship between the thinker, scholar, and citizen.

The Endowment is a federal agency, created by the Congress in 1965. It awards fellowships and research grants for work in the humanities, supports improvements in formal education in the humanities, and funds programs to make the humanities more accessible to the general public.